WHAT'S IN A NAME

Rediscovering the Integrity of God

Fay Rowe

WHAT'S IN A NAME?
Rediscovering the Integrity of God

By Fay Rowe
Copyright © 2007, Fay Rowe

ISBN # 1-897373-06-6

All scriptures, unless otherwise noted, are from The Authorized King James Version, The World Publishing Company, Cleveland and New York, 1945. Used by permission.

Scripture quotations marked "NKJV™" are taken from the New King James Version®. Copyright © 1982 by Thomas Nelson, Inc. Used by permission. All rights reserved.

The Interlinear Hebrew-Aramaic Old Testament by Jay P. Green (ed.). Copyright ©1961 by Hendrickson Publishers, Peabody, Massachusetts. Used by permission. All rights reserved.

"September 11" from TEN MINUTES FROM NORMAL by Karen Hughes. Copyright © 2004 by Karen Hughes. Used by permission of Viking Penguin, a division of Penguin Group (USA) Inc.

THE VOYAGE OF THE DAWN TREADER by C.S. Lewis copyright © C.S. Lewis Pte. Ltd. 1952. Extract reprinted by permission.

Published by Word Alive Press
131 Cordite Road, Winnipeg, Manitoba, Canada R3W 1S1

WORD ALIVE PRESS

DEDICATION

To Emmie

Emmie Louise Evans, my sister, went to Heaven in the early morning hours of May 8, 1985. A beautiful physical presence whose loving spirit exuded joy, intelligence, fun-filled chaos, and yet, amazingly, peace, she could fill a room with electrifying energy, and bring to that same room a warmth and comfort like that of a glowing fire. An empty space remains in the hearts and lives of all who knew her; but still, we were blessed. Our greatest sadness is for those who didn't get to share her light.

On the day I was told of her emergency surgery and dreadful diagnosis, I reached for my Bible with shaking heart and hands. Too distraught for tears I prayed, "God, I need to know how to deal with this. I'm going to read this book as if I've never seen it before, and I want you to talk to me through it!"

That moment changed me from someone who thought she knew all that God was willing to let us know about Himself and His ways, to someone who recognized her own debilitating ignorance and lack of understanding. Ever since then, this verse from Proverbs 4:7 refuses to be put to bed: *"With all thy getting, get understanding."*

This book is just one result of what happened that day.

ACKNOWLEDGEMENTS

There are many whom I need to thank for their remarkable generosity of both heart and effort which helped and encouraged me as I wrote this book. There are too many, in fact, to include every name in this space, but there are some I must mention.

First, there is Nadine, the young woman who didn't know she gave me a gentle push toward writing this book when she casually joked after my farewell talk to the ladies' group at the church I attended before moving to London, "We'll miss you. We'll support your ministry. We'll buy your books." Thank you, Nadine Matthews, for planting the seed!

My long time friend, Diann Vail, and her eclectic group of women friends were a catalyst in the mix that produced this undertaking. I'll always remember the Christmas party my first year in London when, as we sat in Diann's living room and I listened to their chatter, I recognized in them the joy to be found in reaching for possibilities. They showed me so clearly that the most regrettable failure is failure to try. Thanks to them all for making me aware my comfort zone was no longer comfortable.

My new friend, Linda Greenberg, critiqued more of the early drafts of this manuscript than friendship would require, and did it with her customary enthusiasm, which, in itself, was somehow empowering to me. My friends, Judy and Glen Smeltzer, who read those same early drafts and suggested they'd like to see the author in the book, were of invaluable support. So also was my friend, Ida Hall, who donated precious time to make sure

I restrained my inclination to overindulge a love of commas!

To Rev. Lorne Rostotski and Dr. Norrel London for their encouragement and kind words of endorsement, and to all the other friends and family for their gentle critiques and insightful suggestions, I give my heartfelt thanks.

Thanks, also, to my pastors, Jay and Sarah Jayaraman, for being such encouragers and examples of obedience.

Finally, where would I be without the unfailing love and support of my fan club, Glenn and Gillian? I can count on them not only for an encouraging pat on the back when I need it, but also for a little shove in the right direction when I'm stalled. In my every challenge and endeavor, they "have my six." From a full heart, I thank them both.

Blessings on you all for sharing your gifts and your time.

TABLE OF CONTENTS

INTRODUCTION

You're never the same after you meet Goliath face to face, eyeball to eyeball.

Yes, he still lives, and we have all met him in one form or another, or will. Our personal Goliath wears different disguises—disease, financial ruin, family crisis—but every one has the face of a terrorist.

Like Goliath in the Bible story our tormenter shows up, sometimes daily, to challenge and mock us. His terrifying taunts ring loudly or whisper menacingly, "I'm bringing you down. There is no hope for you. You are helpless." Sometimes, like all but one of the children of Israel, we're convinced Goliath is right. After all, compared to giants we're just—we think—grasshoppers, and who has ever known a grasshopper to kill a giant? We want nothing more than to run and hide to avoid having precious life squished like an insect under those massive feet. But we aren't going anywhere. We're paralyzed, perhaps waiting for a David to show up and take out the troublemaker.

There's no doubt about it; we're all too familiar with giants. But giants aren't the only troublemakers we encounter in life. We also face mountains, towering and black, that stand between where we are and where we need to be. Not as seriously, nor immediately, threatening as the giants, mountains are still daunting prospects; the sight of them can make us heart-and-stomach sick. Sometimes the biggest, most disheartening mountain of all is that we simply can't muster the courage to follow a God-given dream. The safe choice, we think, is to stay right where we are and leave the mountains to mountain climbers. After all, mountains are no place for people like us who are afraid of heights and the dark.

What I've just described is common to all God's children. All of us who have walked a few miles on this earth have faced, and will face, circumstances where our confidence is challenged, not only our confidence in ourselves but also our confidence in God. We may be embarrassed by our struggle; after all, God said He didn't give us a spirit of fear, but here we are, shaking in our shoes!

We may even wonder if God is paying attention to what we're going through. I remember praying while perched precariously halfway up one of my life's mountains, "God, you see where I am, don't you?"

Even though we believe God is watching with loving concern, sometimes we still aren't sure He'll get involved to help us. While we're singing "O God Our Help in Ages Past," we don't dare expect any real help in the present! Maybe we don't want to be presumptuous, or perhaps we just don't want to be disappointed.

This book is about one of the greatest reasons that exist for faith in the promises of God. This reason for believing is as important as our knowledge of God's power, and as precious as our assurance of His love for us. It is crucial that we be convinced of it because if we aren't, even our knowledge of His power and love will not be sufficient to build in us a strong faith. This book is about God's integrity.

If we're reflective and honest, many of us will admit that our perception of God's integrity has been at worst nonexistent and at best perverted. Our hope in Him has been tempered with an unhealthy dose of what we call realism. We rarely expect Him to do what He says.

Even though we would probably hate to admit something like that, even to ourselves, sometimes what's in our heart slips into our conversations: I remember hearing a well-known Christian television personality say that the promise in Acts 16:31, "Believe on the Lord Jesus Christ and thou shalt be saved," was "the only promise God guarantees to fulfill."

The only one? I was shocked when I heard it. I thought, surely, I had heard wrong. Then he said it again. The only one!

Is that what we really believe? Do we really suppose that all the other promises are not quite as dependable as that one? Why would we think that?

If we really do believe that, then somewhere along the way God's character has been maligned and we have neither been aware of it happening nor conscious of its effect on us. The purpose of this book is to help us re-examine how we see God; its lofty goal is to help us see Him more clearly, know His integrity and trust Him again.

PART ONE:

God's Integrity

CHAPTER ONE

HIDDEN TREASURE:
The Magnified Word

*"I will worship toward thy holy temple,
and praise thy name for thy loving kindness
and for thy truth: for thou hast magnified thy
word above all thy name." ~ Psalm 138:2*

1.

"IF ANYONE KNOWS, PLEASE TELL ME"

THERE IT WAS AGAIN, that little annoyance that accompanied the giant. No threatening footfalls, no clanging armor, it was just three simultaneous and almost imperceptible little thunks as new numbers took their place. Breaking the night's silence, the deceptively innocent-looking but surely demonized digital clock purposely, I imagined, irritated and unnerved me. Every hour on the hour it taunted me in triplicate, reminding me I was still awake and daring me to look and see how much—or little—of the night was left. I tried to ignore it. Made a valiant effort.

But here's the annoying thing about clocks, demonized or otherwise: A clock in the middle of an otherwise silent night has the same ability to demand attention as does a phone at any hour of the day. In a deplorably short time, which evidenced the weakness of my will, the sinister power of that clock compelled me to open one eye to see what hour it was now. It was three a.m. As my nights went of late, this one was still pitifully young. I was at the end of my first month of chemotherapy, and sleep was but a beautiful memory.

Before I started chemo, I thought losing my hair would be the hardest thing to endure—vain creature that I am—but it wasn't. There was, after all, an upside to the tragedy: there were no more bad hair days and, thanks to God and good genes, a nicely shaped head made baldness bearable. No, the nausea was, unquestionably, the worst of it, and after that, the anti-nausea drugs.

I had a complicated love-hate relationship with the drugs. I dearly loved them because they killed the nausea; fervently hated them because they stole my sleep. Of course, I had the option of sleeping pills to combat the insomnia, but they had their own less than agreeable side effect which made the gallon of water I had to drink taste like gun metal, or at least what I imagine liquid gun metal would taste like. The water kept the chemotherapy concoction from ruining my bladder, so "to drink or not to drink" was not in question, especially since my 23-year-old daughter— How did her father and I raise such a bully?—stood over me until I drank every drop. No, drinking was not optional.

Pick your battles, they say, so from that delightful array of nausea, bladder disease, gun metal flavoring, or insomnia, I picked insomnia. And here I was, wide-eyed at 3 a.m., communing bitterly with a clock.

It looked as if sleep was going to elude me again tonight, so instead of just lying there meditating on my misery, I inched my way out of bed. I could get up now without throwing up; you know: The Drugs. Then gingerly, quietly, so as not to disturb my husband, I put a teaching tape on the player by my bed.

The tape was entitled *Strengthen Yourself in the Lord.* I had listened to it many times since my ordeal began so I knew it would tell me the story of David and his men returning from battle only to find their wives and children taken captive. Heartbroken, the distraught husbands and fathers "cried their eyes out" and then, human nature being what it is, looked for someone to blame. Of course, David was the front running candidate.

Poor David! He was already having a bad day and now it looked as if it were about to get worse. I guess some might say he was experiencing an extended trial period in his life: he was still dealing with that on going King Saul problem; his fair weather friends, the Philistines, didn't want him around anymore; his own family had been captured; and now, this! Even David's closest friends and companions had turned on him and were about to stone him to death—a definite downturn in an already messy situation!

David had reason to be discouraged and maybe even terrified, and no doubt he was. At that moment, he had a perfect opportunity to become depressed and give up. No one would blame him. After all, how much could one man be expected to endure? But you have to love this about David: he refused to give up. The story tells us he "encouraged himself in the Lord his God." (1 Samuel 30:6)

That's why I put that particular tape on. Not because I was bored or because misery loves company (although the tape would have helped with either of those since the speaker was entertaining and David's troubles more than rivaled my own), it was because the yawning pit of self pity was too close for comfort, and I refused to fall into it. It was going to be a long night, and I needed to find a safer place to spend my time. I needed to do what David did. I had to remind myself, yet again, of the Lord's presence in my own situation because—no matter the popular opinion—what misery really wants, and needs, is hope.

Before long, the preacher's voice began to have a sedating effect and I could sense blissful oblivion or even sweet dreams in the offing. I was happily nodding off when, from somewhere outside my half-drowse, I heard Pastor Bill Johnson from Bethel Church in Redding, California, say to his congregation, "God has magnified His word above all His name." Then, almost as if compelled to be honest, he added this afterthought,

"... and I don't even know what that means. If any of you know, please tell me."

My eyes popped open. How had I missed that before? What an odd request for a preacher to make! I was intrigued. I had found a truth chaser!

TRUTH CHASERS AND TREASURE HUNTERS

I will admit truth chasers can be—and often are—excruciatingly annoying. In fact, they probably should have some sort of self-help group just to deal with the annoying part. However, if there were such a group, I'm sure its membership roster would be quite long because even though at times truth chasers seem to be an endangered species, if they all came out of the closet we might discover they are not all that rare.

In fact, you're probably reading this book because you, too, are a truth chaser.

Not to worry; truth chasing is innate to humans. We all entered this world as truth chasers. Listen to any little one who has just uttered his or her first word. Pretty soon after that first sweet "Dada" or "Mama," we hear a baby's version of "What's that?" At first, the parents of the little darling don't seem to tire of answering that eternal question, but a couple of years go by, the new question is "Why?" and by now the parents tire quickly. Later still, school teachers have a schedule to keep and question periods have a time limit, so before long, sadly, the fledgling truth chaser learns to stop chasing.

To the more cynical observers among us it would seem as though life, as early as possible, gathers its forces to teach these two lessons: first, Questioning too much, or too often, is in poor taste and downright annoying; and second, The need to know is just for a select few. For those of us who don't learn quickly enough, the lesson is repeated fairly often.

I remember an incident that took place back when I was in my twenties. I was attending a church on the west coast of Canada and, after a Bible study one night, I asked my pastor why John the Baptist was beheaded in prison whereas Peter was set free. I thought it was a reasonable question. Since knowledge is power, I figured if Peter knew something that John didn't, I would like to know what it was. After all, it couldn't hurt to know how to deal with trouble without literally losing one's head!

My pastor had no answer for me except "It was God's will," and although he was kind and patient in his response, I came away with the vague feeling that I had done something wrong. I felt as though I had just—as Texans say when they've embarrassed themselves—ripped my britches!

I hesitate to tell this second story of squelched truth-chasing because I'm not proud of it. The incident took place one Sunday, soon after the Bible study episode. We had a guest speaker, a luminary from our denomination's head office, who preached on Hebrews 11:1, "Now faith is the substance of things hoped for, the evidence of things not seen." He was a persuasive speaker and it was a well delivered sermon about how calling to mind what God has done in the past will bolster our expectations of His future blessings. All true, but as he read his text, he changed it to "faith is the *result* of the substance of things hoped for. "

I was disturbed! In my youthful arrogance—That's my story: I'll blame it on my youth!—and no doubt the contention born of that, I marched up to the front of the church after the service to ask why he felt he could insert the words "result of" into that verse. It seemed to me that "the substance" and "the result of the substance" were two different things, and faith couldn't be both. I asked—as innocently as I could—if, maybe, he was really talking about how experience builds hope, and if so, weren't there other scriptures he could use, for example Romans 5:5. If not that, then was it perhaps that he was giving us a clearer translation of Hebrews 11:1 based on his knowledge of the original language?

To this day, I think my question was sweeter than his response, which was less than gracious. But then, it may be that my sin was greater than his. I apologized later. He was, after all, a guest at our church and my pastor's friend, so I realized that an apology was in order, especially since in our earlier conversation I had sort of accused him of insulting the intelligence of the whole congregation by twisting scripture.

My apology predictably met with the same grace as did my question: I recall something about my not being the first woman to attack him. Luckily, I was sufficiently chagrinned by my earlier behavior that I didn't voice what popped into my head: "I'm sure I won't be the last!" Small victory, but it helped; I felt better—redeemed, somehow, from my earlier transgression by resisting this new temptation. (Not theologically correct, I know. I'm not suggesting good works are redemptive: I'm just telling you how I felt.)

The outcome of it all: I learned that, even when you're in your twenties, questioning is still in poor taste and is still annoying.

Okay, I'll admit it. My question in that instance could easily have been mistaken for—or maybe even accurately identified as—a poorly disguised criticism, and therefore would rightly be considered in poor taste. And certainly annoying! Mea culpa. My sin was, indeed, greater than his.

Breast smiting aside, no matter which of us owned the greater fault that day, I walked away from the encounter wondering if there might actually be a universal truth that I hadn't yet clued into, one that said:

Some things in the Bible are just not meant to be understood. And then, this law: Don't ask!

Truthfully and thankfully, I don't think I was convinced of either, even though for quite a few years after that—in fact, until the day mentioned in my dedication—I set aside the chase in favor of the fulfilling busyness of family life, career, and church service. Most of my fellow disciples of Jesus seemed to do the same—or, at least, that's how it looked to me. Our lives were full of fairly worthy occupations— working whatever job was our lot; training, feeding, clothing, and chauffeuring children; singing in the choir; teaching Sunday school and doing many other tasks, tedious or fun, such as shopping, cooking, cleaning, decorating, and entertaining. Of course, there were church services and Bible studies, but it seemed to me that we weren't truth chasers there either. Maybe we were just too tired!

In retrospect, it seems that whenever we gave thought to truth it was from the point of view that we had attained its entirety and all that was needed was that we be motivated enough to live it. There was no need, we assumed, for further illumination. Perhaps we obeyed a vaguely perceived, but definitely unspoken, rule that said we shouldn't go looking for any! (That statement should not be taken as an indictment of either my denomination or my local church. It may not even be an accurate assessment of what was happening in my peers' lives during that time. It is merely my recollection of how I was feeling.)

I guess that's why, even all these years later, Bill Johnson's request intrigued me, "If you know what the magnified word means, tell me." As he quoted Psalm 138:2, he obviously thought he should be able to understand what that verse was telling him, but didn't.

Perhaps even more amazing was the fact that he didn't
seem to mind letting his listeners know he didn't!

I realize some true-hearted and honest believers
might not think it necessary to understand what God did
when He "magnified His word." They might say it's
only important that He did it. After all, they would
reason, we don't need to know what the electrician did
when he wired our house; it's just important that it's
done.

That may be fine when it comes to house wiring,
but when it comes to knowledge of God, it truly is not
fine. David, who wrote the worship song where this
phrase is found, knew exactly what God had done.
Because of it, he says, he worshiped and praised God for
His loving kindness and truth. What if we knew what
David knew? Might it have the same effect on us? If we
could grasp what God did when He magnified his word
above all His name, might we be convinced—as was
David—of God's loving kindness and His truth? And
might, then, our praise and worship be just as heartfelt
as David's?

Maybe it's worth a question or two.

We must never be afraid to question. Questioning is
often necessary because understanding, itself, is crucial.
The Bible says so. Matthew 13:19 records a
conversation Jesus had with His disciples during which
he talked about the subject, "When one hears the word
of the kingdom, and understands it not, then cometh the
wicked one, and catches away that which was sown in
his heart."

Apparently, God's word is less likely to be stolen if
it is understood! Could understanding, therefore, *be*
more important? There should be no wonder that
Proverbs 4:7 instructs us to "with all thy getting, get
understanding." In Proverbs 3:13-14 we see that "happy
is the man who gets understanding, for the merchandise

of it is better than the merchandise of silver and the gain thereof than fine gold." Not just gold, mind you; fine gold! These verses imply that understanding, like gold, will be of immense benefit to one who possesses it, not only because of its beauty but also because of what it will allow its possessor to accomplish.

For too long, I had no understanding of the truth hidden in the last phrase of Psalm 138:2. I had always assumed the phrase meant God's word was important to Him and should be to me also, but I had no idea if it had some specific significance other than giving us a vague sense of the value God placed on His word. Sadly, because I didn't immediately comprehend what it was saying, I ignored it and focused instead on the "loving kindness and truth" part. The Bible was telling me that God has magnified His word above all His name, and I didn't even ask, "So what?" Meanwhile, a nugget of truth lay there undiscovered, like gold on an unexplored riverbed.

On that sleepless night in February when I heard what Bill Johnson said, I knew he had caught sight of that glimmer of gold, and I remembered the day I first saw it. As I lay there reliving "The Day of the Glimmer," I found the encouragement I was looking for.

THE DAY OF THE GLIMMER
(FAKE PRAISE AND TRUE ADVENTURE.)

I love the psalms. Maybe we all do, probably because we see our lives and ourselves reflected in them. Whenever I read what the psalmists wrote about their experiences, I easily identify with their struggles. There's something very familiar about their cries for help mingled with their assertions of, and thanks for, God's faithfulness. I love the fact that as I witness their sometimes failing, but always renewed, hope in God's goodness, I experience that renewal with them. Always, the ancient songs of these very human praisers turn my own eyes back to the one from whom "my help cometh" and inspire me to hope and faith—often just when I am most desperately in need of both!

Some years ago, I began to read aloud from the psalms occasionally during my personal devotions. On The Day of the Glimmer, I was sitting on my bed reading Psalm 138, and I had just declared from verse two, "I thank you that you have magnified your word above all your name," when I stopped, embarrassed. Britches ripped again! I thank you for what?

Suddenly, no doubt a result of my fertile imagination, this disconcerting picture flashed into my mind: God listening intently and knowing that I had no idea what I was saying! I was embarrassed, and I should have been. Did I really think I could impress God by spouting lovely words when He knew I didn't have a clue what they meant? In my flight of fancy His eyes were sad, and I thought I knew the reason. My words must sound terribly hollow to someone who knew not only the words of my mouth before they were spoken but also what was going on in my heart. It was a troubling thought!

I have to admit this next step was taken more to cover my embarrassment than for any other reason. Just in case He really was listening, I prayed sheepishly, "Father, I don't know what that means. Could you show me?"

I had discovered by now that if I asked God for understanding of scripture, I would eventually get my answer from my pastor's sermons, from a teacher on television, from a book, or even from a friend over a steaming cup at Starbuck's. However, this time illumination didn't come from any of these sources.

Every time I read Psalm 138:2 after that day, I prayed the same prayer again, perhaps because whenever I read it I was embarrassed all over again about that "meaningless praise" incident. As weeks and then months passed, my motivation for the prayer changed. My embarrassment was replaced by dogged determination. The reason: I became convinced that the information about God that was held in that little verse was an important key to my understanding "the loving kindness and truth" of God, and there was something about that loving kindness that I needed to know! There was gold in them thar' hills, and I planned to find it.

"You have not because you ask not" was not going to apply to me in this case! I had heard sermons based on Mark 7:7 "Ask (and keep on asking) and it shall be given you; seek (and keep on seeking) and ye shall find." Mark's record of Jesus words showed me that God likes questions and doesn't mind a nag. Good to know!

So I nagged.

Finally, one day, as I prayed yet again, "Lord, I don't understand how you can magnify your word above your name, but your Holy Spirit is my teacher and I thank you that He will show me what it means," I had this thought: You know what the word is; study the name.

What did the name mean? I felt as if I were being sidetracked from my objective. After all, I was curious about the magnified word, not the name. But, then, what did I have to lose? At least I was on the move!

This verse from Proverbs told me what my first step must be:

Proverbs 2:1-5, "My son, if thou wilt receive my words, and hide my commandments with thee; So that thou incline thine ear unto wisdom, and apply thine heart to understanding; yea, if thou cryest after knowledge, and liftest up thy voice for understanding; if thou seekest for her as for silver, and searchest for her as for hid treasures; then shalt thou understand the fear of the Lord and find the knowledge of God."

As I read those words, I suddenly flashed back to the dusty grounds of Camp Emmanuel, the church camp that gave me the best two weeks of summer vacation for most of my formative years. Nestled on a hill and valley on Canada's east coast, on the island of Newfoundland, the cluster of cabins, dorms, diner, tabernacle, and unforgettable outhouses overlooked the shining waters of Conception Bay, where the air was the sweetest breathed on God's earth.

In my reverie, I held the autograph book I had bought at the Book Nook's Last Day Sale to catch those "last words" from my new and old friends before we headed home. There on its pastel pages—between the "Friends 4 ever" over one friend's name and address, and the "2 sweet 2 be 4 gotten" penned by another—my Daily Vacation Bible School teacher had scrawled a Bible verse. He had written simply, "Study to show thyself approved unto God, a workman that needeth not to be ashamed, rightly dividing the word of truth," 2 Timothy 2:15, and signed his name, Lindahl Faulkner.

That scene had taken place in the sixties. Now, years later, I could still remember the slight feeling of uneasiness I'd had as I read his words. Lindahl, whose impact on me can be measured by the fact that he's the only DVBS teacher whose face I can clearly recall, had spent two weeks teaching from book of Jude and had taken every opportunity to remind us that we had been handed a wonderful treasure, the "faith once delivered to the saints." With fire in his eyes, he daily challenged us to handle this treasure with care.

Looking back now, I realize that my uneasiness about what he had written came from the fact that I subscribed to the "I don't cuss and I don't chew, and I don't kiss the boys that do" brand of Christianity, otherwise known, when one becomes proficient, as "Miss Goody Two Shoes Syndrome." In other words, I would try to live as good a life as I knew how and just hope that my effort would bring me whatever approval I needed.

The tenets of faith to which my denomination held included salvation by grace, but, somehow, I didn't quite grasp, back then, that I had been approved of God the moment I had accepted Jesus' sacrifice for my sin. That may have been because the youth leaders during my teen years—Lindahl being a notable exception—no doubt in an honest and honorable effort to encourage young believers to make right decisions, focused a great deal on what actions would, or would not, be pleasing to God. Perhaps as a result of that, I confused the notion of "actions that were pleasing to God because they were right," with "actions that were right because they were pleasing to God," and from there developed my own concept of "salvation by works." Consequently, to my mind, the verse Lindahl had written in my autograph book read, "Study so that God will approve you." In my ignorance or, more accurately, my confusion, I felt this admonition from the book of Timothy gave me another requirement I had to meet for my salvation, and I knew I would fall short. I hated the shame of falling short; hence, the uneasiness.

Now, many years later—in Proverbs this time— here it was again: a challenge to engage. I knew the "if" part of Proverbs 2 was my responsibility. "Receive my words. Put your heart in it. Listen. Ask. Seek. Search!" No one could do it for me, and I would go no further without this step!

This time, however, I knew the purpose of the challenge wasn't to gain approval but, rather, to gain a very precious commodity: understanding—the kind God gives. Life had already shown me how precious and how very necessary it is. This time, too, I understood the fire I had seen decades ago in my teacher's eyes, and the challenge brought no uneasiness. Instead, there was only anticipation of something good. There was hidden treasure to be uncovered; silver and gold to be found.

Proverbs called me to an adventure, a search for the treasure in Psalm 138:2.

Now, having picked up this book, you've been called to the same adventure!

Thomas Cahill, in his book *How the Irish Saved Civilization*, describes St. Augustine's conversion to Christianity. There, Cahill tells how Augustine began to read Paul's writings and came to the conclusion that "if we mud-spattered human beings are ever to ascend to Truth, we can do it only because God, a force greater than our war-torn selves, has predestined us and calls us upward."

Be assured He calls us upward.

Thinking About Chapter One

SELF DISCOVERY QUESTIONS:

1. What does Psalm 138:2 mean to you?

2. Do you feel uneasy about being called to this adventure? If so, why?

3. Are you willing to take this journey?

TRUTH CHASER'S PRAYER:

Father God,

Please wake up the truth chaser in me. Help me to hear Your call to search for truth, and help me always to be willing to go on this journey with You. Thank You for the guidance which comes so faithfully from Your Holy Spirit. And, thank You, ahead of time, for being patient with me!

CHAPTER TWO

THEY THAT
KNOW THY NAME

"It is not the critic who counts; not the man who points out where the strong man stumbles or where the doer of deeds could have done them better. The credit belongs to the man who is actually in the arena, whose face is marred by dust and sweat and blood: who strives valiantly; who errs, and comes short again and again; because there is not effort without error and shortcoming; but who does actually strive to do the deeds; who knows the great enthusiasms, the great devotions; who spends himself in a worthy cause, who at the best knows in the end the triumphs of high achievement and who at the worst, if he fails, at least fails while daring greatly, so that his place shall never be with those cold and timid souls who know neither victory or defeat."

THEODORE ROOSEVELT
Speech: The Man In The Arena
Sorbonne, April 23, 1910.

2.

"They that know thy name will put their trust in thee, for thou Lord hast not forsaken them that seek thee." ~Psalm 9:10

THERE IT WAS—a signpost: Psalm 9:10.

Apparently, according to Psalm 9:10, knowing God's name is a confidence builder. It follows, therefore, that people who know God's name carry an identifying trademark: trust in God. It occurred to me that in studying some people who displayed confidence in God I would find out what they knew about Him—or about His name—that so affected their level of trust. I figured if I could walk with some of them through their most challenging experiences, watch them carefully, and listen intently to what they had to say, I might find out exactly what did motivate and empower them.

There are more than a few examples of such people in the Bible. Abraham quickly came to mind, as did King David and the three Hebrew children. Although the acts for which we remember them were definitely out of the ordinary, and, no doubt, brought them a few critics at the time, it was pretty clear to me that they all trusted God and set their hope in Him; so, according to my signpost, they must have known God's name. I decided they would be suitable mentors or models for me in my search for knowledge of "the name."

ABRAHAM'S STORY

One of Abraham's stories is told in Genesis 22. God had given Abraham a son and had told him, "In Isaac shall thy seed be called." In other words, the promise God had given Abraham—that he would be a father of many nations—would be fulfilled through Isaac. Surprisingly, we later hear God telling Abraham to sacrifice Isaac as a burnt offering in the land of Moriah. Isaac, the son of promise, was to be killed on an altar!

Tradition suggests that this command to sacrifice Isaac was a test of Abraham's love, obedience, or commitment to the Lord, and of course, he passed.

All right, then, let's watch closely. Just how did Abraham respond to God's command? How did he pass what must have been a profoundly painful test? Where did he find the strength to obey?

Hebrews 11: 17-19 tells us about what was going on in Abraham's mind and heart.

"By faith Abraham, when he was tried, offered up Isaac: and he that received the promises offered up his only begotten son, Of whom it was said, That in Isaac shall thy seed be called: accounting that God was able to raise him up, even from the dead; from whence he received him in a figure."

It would seem that Abraham expected God to bring Isaac back from the dead!

One morning during a devotional at a Christian high school, I talked about Abraham's amazing expectation. I was very surprised when I received a strong negative response from one of the students. He was appalled that I would suggest that Abraham's obedience could have been influenced by anything other than love for God and absolute self-sacrifice. He couldn't believe that Abraham expected God to raise Isaac from the dead— even though the book of Hebrews suggests he did! Not only does Hebrews suggest it, but Abraham's own words to his servants also indicate as much. Before he left them, Abraham said, "I and the lad will go yonder and worship, and come to you again." Unless he was lying to his servants, Abraham expected Isaac to return with him.

Taken aback by my student's response, I wondered for some time why this devout and intelligent young man was so vehement in his refusal to accept that Abraham's knowledge of God led him to believe God would raise Isaac from the dead. He refused to accept it even in the face of strong Biblical evidence.

I finally came to the conclusion that it may have been because it is easier for us to try to emulate Father Abraham's willingness to sacrifice his best for God than it is to share his absolute belief that God would fulfill his promises—in this case the one that said "in Isaac shall thy seed be called,"—even in the face of apparent denial of that very promise.

Abraham continued to believe God's promise about Isaac even in the face of Isaac's imminent demise at his father's own hand. We, on the other hand, often back down when confronted with circumstances that conflict with the promises given to us. Why do we do that? Why are we so quick to let go of specific promises God has made? Or why do we find it difficult to hold fast to them confidently?

Today, we have a written record of the many promises of God. We have read the account of the extent to which God went to redeem us, sacrificing His son, Jesus, on the cross, all because of His great love for us. We don't doubt His love. Yet, we sometimes struggle to believe that these promises made by our greatest lover will be fulfilled.

What did Father Abraham know that we don't know? Why should he expect, if indeed he did, that God would give him back his son? Did he, perhaps, know something about the "magnified word" mentioned in Psalm 138?

DAVID'S STORY

In the first book of Samuel, chapter 17 tells what is probably the most famous of David's stories. It happened when David was still a young man, long before anyone sang songs of his bravery and skill in battle. His father had sent him to take food to his brothers who were at the battle site where the Philistines and their trump card, the formidable warrior-giant, Goliath, held King Saul and the men of Israel at a standstill.

As a shepherd, young David had spent much time on the hillsides caring for his father's sheep. No doubt, during long days and nights when the quiet was interrupted only by the bleating of the sheep and the occasional pesky predator, he meditated on the God of his fathers. We can confidently assume David spent considerable time thinking about God on those hills, not only because we know the many worship songs he wrote during those days, but also because we can see that his fathers' God immediately came to mind when he saw what was going on in the valley of Elah that day.

Listen to this youngster:

Vs 26: "Who is this uncircumcised Philistine, that he should defy the armies of the living God?"

Hear the outrage in his voice!

David saw the men of Israel cowering in the presence of trouble and knew there was something very wrong with this scene. Here was the problem: this man, Goliath, was uncircumcised. He, therefore, had no covenant with God. God had made him no promises.

Yet, here in this valley, the children of Israel, who were the possessors of the promises, were the fearful ones!

It was unthinkable; David knew it just shouldn't be. He began to speak out—quite annoyingly, I imagine—to everyone around him, "God will deliver us from this scourge!"

His older brother scolded him for his insolence and presumption, to which spunky young David replied, "What have I done? Is there not a cause?" David was saying, "Don't I have reason to say these things, considering our covenant?"

The fiery young shepherd preached his message to all who would listen to him, and finally the soldiers took him to King Saul himself. With vivid accounts of his past victories by God's hand—such as the stories about the lions and bears that tried and failed to steal his sheep—David attempted to persuade Saul to let him face the bone-chilling Goliath.

Miracle of miracles, it worked!

I've often wondered what Saul saw in David's eyes or heard in his voice that made him decide to send him out—a boy against a giant, a singing shepherd against a proven warrior. Whatever it was, I'll bet Goliath, too, saw it in David's fearless run toward him on the field of battle and heard it in his shouted declaration: "You came to me with a sword, and with a spear, and with a shield: but I come to you in the name of the Lord of hosts, the God of the armies of Israel, whom thou hast defied" (Vs: 45).

Why such bravado? Could it simply be that just like Abraham, who had the word of the Lord that assured him Isaac would be the one from whom his progeny would spring, David had a promise that he expected to be fulfilled?

David certainly would have known that deliverance from their enemies was one of God's promises to His people. Deuteronomy 28:7 says, "The Lord shall cause thine enemies that rise up against thee to be smitten before thy face: they shall come out against thee one way, and flee before thee seven ways."

Israel's covenant promised them smitten enemies. David knew that. Could that be why he knew he would smite Goliath that day? Listen to what he confidently yelled to the threatening Goliath in verse 46: "This day will the Lord deliver thee into mine hand; and I will smite thee."

In this one amazing statement I hear young David's confidence that God would uphold the words recorded in Deuteronomy 28: "thine enemies…smitten before thy face."

This same verse told him his enemies would flee before him seven ways.

Well, did David's enemies flee? Indeed they did. Verse 51 tells us, "and when the Philistines saw their champion was dead, they fled." Imagine that!

THE THREE HEBREW CHILDREN'S STORY

The story of Shadrach, Meshach, and Abednego, is told in chapter three of the book of Daniel.

Daniel 3:14-18.

14 Nebuchadnezzar spoke and said unto them, Is it true, O Shadrach, Meshach, and Abednego, do not ye serve my gods, nor worship the golden image which I have set up?
15 Now if ye be ready that at what time ye hear the sound of the cornet, flute, harp, sackbut, psaltry, and dulcimer, and all kinds of music, ye fall down and worship the image I have made, well: but if ye worship not, ye shall be cast the same hour into the midst of a fiery furnace; and who is that God that shall deliver you out of my hands?

16 Shadrach, Meshach, and Abednego, answered and said to the king, O Nebuchadnezzar, we are not careful to answer thee in this matter.

17 *If it be so*, our God whom we serve is able to deliver us from the burning fiery furnace, and he will deliver us out of thine hand, O king.

18 *But if not*, be it known unto thee, O king, that we will not serve thy gods, nor worship the golden image which thou hast set up.

We love the rest of the story. They were thrown into the flames, but suddenly, miraculously, they were joined by a big fellow who looked so powerful he appeared to be "like the son of God," and, wonder of wonders, the four of them walked freely in the fire.

When the king saw this, he had an immediate conversion experience. Not surprising, since when one who looks like the son of God shows up in a conflict, you definitely want to be found on his side! Whatever Nebuchadnezzar's motivation, whether change of heart or survival instinct, he altered his furnace policy. Listen to him as he tells our sweet-smelling, no-smoke-on-them young heroes to "come hither" out of the fire.

Vs 28: Then Nebuchadnezzar spake and said, Blessed be the God of Shadrach, Mechach, and Abednego, who hath sent his angel, and delivered his servants that trusted in him...and yielded their bodies that they might not serve nor worship any god except their own God.

In this case, as with Abraham, God delivered His children even when it looked as if all hope was lost!

This familiar story has often been taught in order to encourage us to be completely dedicated and obedient to God, even in the face of adversity. Such dedication and obedience are admirable, to be sure, and necessary, without doubt. However, sometimes we have been led,

incorrectly, to believe that those three brave boys went
into the flames thinking God might not help them. A
common misconception, this idea comes from the words
recorded in verse 18 when the boys said to the king,
"Our God will deliver us...but if not, we will not serve
your gods."

But that, in fact, is not what this passage is saying.
Others may have thought hope was lost, but not these
young Hebrews. If we listen to them very carefully we
realize that these boys were actually convinced that God
would deliver them.

See here what the boys were really thinking, and
saying:

> Vs 17: "*If it be so*, our god whom we serve is able
> to deliver us from the fiery furnace, and he will
> deliver us out of thine hand O king."

If what be so? If the king's threat be so! These boys
were actually saying they doubted the king's ability to
carry out his threat! Here's the king's threat:

> Vs 15: "If ye worship not, ye shall be cast that same
> hour into the midst of a burning fiery furnace."

So, in verse 17, the boys are telling the king that if he
throws them in, "our God *can* and *will* deliver us out of
your hand." According to this, they didn't doubt either
God's ability or His willingness to deliver them!

Let's look at verses 17 and 18 together:

> "*If it be so* (that is, if you throw us in the furnace)
> our God *can* and *will* deliver us from your hand.
> *But if not* (that is, if you do not throw us in the
> furnace), we still will not bow down and worship
> the image."

In other words: "No negotiation! No deal! No way!"

Why would these three Hebrews say "Our God will deliver us" as well as "Our God can deliver us"? We remember, of course, that they had heard the stories of the great deliverances of the past and had seen the hand of God deliver their people more than once. History told them God could deliver, but what made them say He will?

It probably was because they knew the scriptures. We can safely assume that they did so because we saw evidence of that fact in their diligent and meticulous efforts to obey the law. Remember, these were the boys who earlier refused to eat the king's food because their covenant told them it was unlawful to do so. Surely, because of their knowledge of their covenant, they also would have known that in Isaiah 43:2 it was recorded that God had said, "When thou passest through the waters I will be with thee: when thou walkest through the fire, thou shalt not be burned; neither shall the flame kindle upon thee."

They probably recalled verses from Psalms that told of God's willingness to deliver all who fear Him. Psalm 34:7, for example, says, "The angel of the Lord encampeth round about them that fear him and delivereth them." The only proviso of this promise was fear of God, and it is apparent from their actions that these young fellows feared God. That's how they got into this trouble in the first place: obedience to God's directive to worship no other gods, an obedience no doubt born out of a proper fear and respect for God.

They knew the commandments; they knew the promises. Is there something else Shadrach, Mechach, and Abednego could have known that would make them say God will, and not just God can? Is it possible these boys are saying, in verse 17, that they, like Abraham and David before them, expected God to do exactly what He said?

Could they have actually expected angels and deliverance? If so, were they merely being presumptuous?

Or is it possible they, like Abraham and David, knew something about the magnified word?

If we knew it, might we, too, be convinced not only of God's right and ability to do what He says but also of His willingness to do what He says?

Many of us know what's been promised to us. We have "exceeding great and precious promises, whereby we are partakers of the divine nature," (2 Peter 1:4). Like David and the three Hebrews, we have heard the stories that have preceded ours over the many generations since the days of Abraham—stories of great exploits done by people who knew their God. Yet, many of us still cower when a giant, someone or some circumstance bigger than us, threatens.

Of course we cower, you say; we're human.

Sure we are. So were they.

In Daniel 11:32, we are told they that know their God will be strong and do exploits. We can probably agree that the few men we have studied here were strong and did exploits. Have you ever wondered why these people, who weren't indwelt by the Holy Spirit, appear stronger than we seem to be—we, who have been given the Comforter? We have a covenant too. A better covenant, we're told, based on better promises. Yet, not many of us can claim the spiritual strength we see in the stories of these people. What might they have known of God? Is it something we haven't known? The Bible tells us in Isaiah 30:15 that in quietness and confidence is our strength. Where did their confidence come from?

I think sometimes, in the telling of these stories to our children in Sunday school, or even in our pulpits to our adult congregations, we tend to make heroes of the men and, really, they did have qualities we recognize as heroic. We admire them for their courage, faith, obedience, and self-sacrifice: all qualities we wish we had. Of course, the stories are told so that we would not only admire, but also imitate them, as indicated in the songs we used to sing in Sunday school, such as *Dare to be a Daniel.* The stories are told to motivate us to be of good courage, to trust God, to be obedient.

All good, if the stories have their intended effect.

However, sometimes instead of being motivated, we're intimidated. Even as you read this, you may be starting to feel a little inadequate in courage, trust, and obedience. Perhaps it is when we feel most inadequate that the "I don't cuss and I don't chew" philosophy appears so attractive. It's much less demanding, we think, than giant slaying.

It certainly is less demanding. It's also less glorious. To my knowledge, there are no songs which celebrate a quite admirable abstinence from cussing and chewing!

Could our focus possibly be off? In our focusing on these wonderful heroes of the faith, is it possible we come away not really seeing the true hero of those stories—our loving, faithful, strong and mighty God? Is there something else we need to know about God before we can be bold and do exploits like the great men of old?

Listen to them again.

Abraham: *"I and the lad will return."*

David: *"This day the Lord will deliver thee into my hand."*

Three Hebrews: *"Our God can and will deliver us."*

Such certainty! Such confidence! Where did it come from?

I've heard it said that these great men of Old Testament times had such boldness and confidence because of a "special" anointing of the Holy Spirit that came upon them to enable them to do something out of the ordinary for God. There have been times when I've wanted to believe that. After all, that would mean my ineffectiveness could be excused by a lack of special anointing, and, I confess, my natural tendency is to opt for any explanations of scripture that leave me in my comfort zone.

If that were true, though, wouldn't the Bible, the book "profitable for doctrine," tell us so? Wouldn't it say of them, as it does of others, that "the spirit of the Lord came upon them and they prophesied" as they declared their victory in advance? One would think it should since the Author is interested in our correct doctrine, but no, it doesn't.

Comfort must always give way to truth, so since there was no such statement about them in these instances, we shouldn't presume that it happened that way!

Well, then, if it wasn't a special anointing that empowered them, what was it that made them do the great exploits we have read about? Did Abraham, David, Shadrach, Meshach, and Abednego simply know, better than we, what a hero God is?

Thinking About Chapter Two

SELF DISCOVERY QUESTIONS:

1. Do you feel you know God's name?

2. Do you have the same confidence in God that the Bible heroes had?

3. Do you think it would it be prideful to say that you had such confidence in God?

4. Are there certain words from God which you have clung to in times of trouble?

TRUTH CHASER'S PRAYER:

Dear Father,

I confess I love my comfort zone. I admit I can't imagine doing anything remotely like the courageous acts I read about in Your word. I can't even imagine You'd want me to do them! But I know there must be something you want me to do. Something good and great. Something I can only do with your help. If so, I may need to know You as David and Abraham did, and as those three young Hebrew boys did. So please help me. Help me to know Your name.

CHAPTER THREE

---•———————————————•---

WHAT'S IN A NAME?

"What's in a name?
That which we call
by any other name
would smell as sweet."

WILLIAM SHAKESPEARE
Romeo and Juliet

3.

" Then they that feared the Lord spake often one to another: and the Lord hearkened, and heard it, and a book of remembrance was written before him for them that feared the Lord, and that thought upon his name, and they shall be mine, saith the Lord of hosts, in that day when I make up my jewels, . . . " ~Malachi 3:16–17

Imagine yourself with the same kind of courage and confidence in God that these men showed. Not possible? It must be! They weren't some super-spiritual breed of men. They must have been ordinary people, just like us, because they certainly had the same human frailties we have.

Pause for a moment and think of David's life. As well as his spiritual, physical, and ethical victories, don't the words "adultery" and "murder" come to mind? You'll no doubt agree that human frailties were David's constant companions.

Abraham's, too. Along with the times Abraham made heroic choices, there were a couple of moments that were remarkable only for their apparent cowardice as he effectively hid behind his wife's skirt tail, presenting her as his sister so no one would kill him in order to have her!

No, theirs was not a special kind of trust that God reserved for, doled out to, or placed in the hearts of a few heroic human beings. Actually, it seems that their heroism sprang from their ability to trust, not the other way around! Psalm 9:10 indicates that this trust was born of their knowledge of God. If the psalmist is to be believed, anyone who knows God's name will trust Him. Anyone!

We all have the same Father God. A businessman from New York has the same Father as an ancient, nomadic new believer from Ur of the Chaldees. A homemaker in Dallas has the same Father as a shepherd on the hills near Bethlehem. An office worker in Toronto has the same Father as three Israeli slaves facing annihilation in the ancient land that is now known as Iraq. Surely, we can all have the same trust in our Father.

Would we, if we really knew His name? Are you ready for the adventure? It begins here.

TRAIL ONE: THE NAMES OF GOD

I had read a few books and heard numerous sermons about the names of God, and those were what first came to mind when I began my study of the name. The names of God which He disclosed to the children of Israel reveal who He is and what He intends His relationship with us to be: Our Shepherd, Righteousness, Healer, Victory, Peace, Ever-present One, and so on. To study these names is to be blessed by the knowledge of God's heart toward His people, the Israelites, and His children, the church.

However, after following that trail for some time, I was no further ahead in my understanding of that scripture in Psalm 138. After all, why would God magnify His word above those names which represent His promised covenant relationship with His children? It is His word that reveals His desire and plan to establish such a relationship with us, so how could His word be exalted above that relationship? It just didn't make sense.

When the Holy Spirit teaches He doesn't leave us wondering, and God's word makes sense. No mental gymnastics or suspension of disbelief on our part is needed when the great Teacher of the church teaches, so I knew this couldn't be the right path.

Daunted for just a moment, I knew there had to be another route, so I kept searching. There had to be another use of the word "name" that would work in that verse and make its meaning clear, and I knew I would find it if I didn't become weary in well doing!

The chase continued on another trail. On this one there is familiar ground, much closer to home for us: What is the significance of any man's name?

TRAIL TWO: ANY MAN'S NAME

When I finally had the thought, "What's in a name?" I began to get excited, because, although I didn't yet know where it would lead, I knew in my heart I was on the right track.

Here's where the journey started: It occurred to me that it was God who gave us the ability to use words and communicates with us through words; it's one way we were made in His image! I also realized that in our tendency to spiritualize Biblical language and, in doing so, remove it from any connection to our every day usage, we may have inadvertently created a hindrance to our understanding.

For those two reasons I decided to examine how the word "name" itself is used in other places in the Bible and in our own daily usage. If I could clarify in my own mind the implications of anyone's name and the different ways the word "name" is used, then, perhaps, I would understand more of what is meant by the name of the Lord. By thus "de-spiritualizing" the word I might possibly shed some light on its use in Psalm 138:2.

This new trail begins as we examine several aspects of one's name and different applications of the word "name." Don't lose heart, brave truth chaser. The treasure is worth the trip!

IDENTIFICATION
"HER NAME IS GILLIAN ELIZABETH."

The scene: Grace Maternity Hospital in Halifax, Nova Scotia. Our beautiful on-time baby daughter had, but an hour or two ago, made her earth debut. Of course, my husband and I were thrilled and wanted to call all our family and friends throughout Canada to tell of her safe arrival. There was, however, a problem: I had convinced myself we were having a boy—a boy whom I had called Richard for many months now. It wasn't that I particularly wanted a boy. In fact, I think I really wanted a girl but pictured a boy so I wouldn't be disappointed if a boy showed up! Whatever the reason, I had imagined a dark haired little Richard and, instead, here was a tiny blonde baby girl. I was thrilled by this development, but I wasn't prepared for it; Richard was the only name we had thought of! And now my husband refused to make a call until she had a name, protesting, "It just doesn't seem right to introduce her without a name." Inspiration came: "She's Gillian Elizabeth." We didn't know it then, but it means youthful downy-haired one, consecrated to God. And so she was, and is.

The first thing a name does is give the simplest of answers to the question, "Who are you?" Identification, or distinction, is the most basic purpose of a name. Historians tell us many of the familiar surnames of our day came about as individuals were identified by the occupation they pursued. Thus, we have John Carpenter, John Farmer or John Smith. When we know two or more people who have the same name, we add something to the names to aid in the distinction. For example, there are John Jones Sr., John Jones Jr., Brother John, or Cousin John.

Even God identified himself to Moses by giving His name. As the story in Exodus goes, God had just instructed Moses to go to His people in Egypt and lead them out. Moses knew that he would be called upon to identify the source of his power. By giving the name of the one who sent him, he would legitimize his claim that he was sent to bring the children of Israel out from Egypt. Moses says, "They'll ask who sent me. They'll say, 'what is his name?'"

The answer came.

Exodus 3:14, "And God said unto Moses, I AM THAT I AM: and he said, Thus shalt thou say unto the children of Israel, 'I AM hath sent me unto you.'"

There, Moses. I AM is backing you up.

CHARACTER
"YOU CAN'T TELL A BOOK BY ITS COVER."

We know it's true: Outward appearances can be deceiving. Even though we often quickly judge someone by his looks, clothing, job, or family name, we all can recognize the folly inherent in that practice. The truth is, if all we know is someone's identity, we still know very little about that person. To really know someone, we need to know his character. However, since we can't see into someone's heart and mind, we determine a person's character through his words and actions.

Proverbs 20:11 says, "Even a child is known by his doings, whether his work be pure, and whether it be right."

We know how it works: when someone's actions result in good for other people, we say he is kind; when someone's words and actions agree we say he has integrity; when someone speaks the truth as he knows it, we say he is honest. On the other hand, if one whom we have known to be honest appears to have lied, we say the action is out of character for that individual. And so it goes!

Psalm 9:16 says, "The Lord is known by the judgment which he executeth."

Even God is known by His actions!

This knowledge of actions and resulting perception of character is part of what creates a reputation, a very important aspect of one's name.

REPUTATION
"YOUR REPUTATION HAS EXCEEDED YOU."

Several years ago, my family and I were members of a church whose pastor traveled quite often in ministry to other churches. On one occasion, he was ministering in one of the largest churches in America. The service was being televised across much of the nation and he had told us, his own church family, to be sure to watch. Of course, we did. When he came to the pulpit in that huge church, in that widely televised service, he tried to tell the congregation how pleased and honored he was to have been invited to minister to them. Obviously intending to say, "Your reputation has preceded you," he said instead, "Your reputation has exceeded you." The following week in our home church, with solemn countenance but with tongue in cheek, he invited the whole church to repent for laughing at him and suggested his wife lead the way!

Proverbs 22:1 refers to this aspect of one's name, "a good name is rather to be chosen than great riches." The message to the angel at the church in Sardis was, "thou hast a name that thou livest, and art dead." (Revelation 3:1) In this case, their reputation really had exceeded them!

We often refer to the reputation of a person, product, company, etc. by the word "name." We might say "Buy good name brands," or "That ministry/person/company has a good name," or perhaps even, "That fellow's name is mud." We don't mean that there is something especially nice or nasty about the word by which they are identified; we are talking about their reputation.

In the business world, marketers are all about reputation. They know the importance of creating the impression that their product is consistently good and therefore worthy of the consumer's trust. That is part of what is known as "branding," and to do so they spend a great deal of their company's resources on everything from packaging and product positioning in the marketplace to advertising campaigns and focus groups who tell them what people think about all of it!

These same marketers are aware of how important it is that production departments keep the highest level of quality control possible so that the product is, in fact, consistently good and all that it claims to be. They know that in spite of all the marketing hype, if there is no substance to the claims made, consumers simply won't believe in the product. They are also aware that when we test a product and find it to be good over a period of time—when it has been tried and, indeed, found to be true—we'll show our trust by our loyalty. We will consistently buy the product because our experience allows us to expect good things from its manufacturer; we will trust that name brand and respond accordingly.

On the other hand, if we have tried the product and found it to be of poor quality, the reputation—the good name—of both the product and the company is then tarnished and we look elsewhere for what we need. Actually, sometimes all that's needed for us to refuse to trust a product or company is a report of someone else's negative experience. That particular company's name, built upon its poor performance, is not good, so it may take some time and forgetfulness for us ever to buy the product, or indeed any product from that manufacturer, again.

Some other aspects that are wrapped up in the reputation of companies or people are power, ability, and even assets. For example, when we hear the names Microsoft, Walmart, or even Tiger Woods, we have a bigger picture than computers, dry goods, or golf, and we have definite expectations of each of them. On the other hand, when we hear the name Johnny Smith, we may have no idea of what to expect from Johnny. If, however, Johnny Smith was known to have great assets, either of accumulated wealth or physical prowess or intellectual ability, his reputation would be affected by that knowledge.

But if Johnny were introduced to us as Johnny Rockefeller, we would immediately think that he has access to resources that will help him achieve greatness. The financial assets available to Johnny would give him the power to do what he wanted to do in life. We might even think that he has genes that could possibly give him abilities above the norm. All this would come to mind because of the reputation already established by someone of that name.

Reputation is powerful! It is so much so that today the concept of branding is not limited to goods and services. Personal branding has come to the forefront in a competitive environment where careers stand or fall on the opinions of others. We all know of people who have deliberately engaged in personal branding for selfish purposes and have given spin doctors a challenging job; eventually, however, the truth does out and these people wear the brand they have earned. There are others, however, whose brand develops naturally over time. One great example among these natural brands is Dr.

Billy Graham. His brand of sincerity, wisdom and integrity has given him the ear of many leaders in the worlds of religion and politics, and has also given him a place of great influence among Christians worldwide.

So what does all this have to do with God's name? Just this: God knew, long before our twenty-first century marketers and publicists, that being known and being positively perceived is important. Psalm 76:1 says, "in Judah God is known: his name is great in Israel." When God truly is known and His character and works reported accurately, then His name, His reputation, is very great!

Because it has always been important to God that He be represented accurately in the earth, He gave specific instructions to the children of Israel to ensure that His reputation would continue to be known. In Psalm 78, we see that the children of Israel were to pass on to their children the reputation of God by telling them about His mighty acts toward His people. In verse 7 we see the reason they were to do it: "that they might set their hope in God, and not forget the works of God, but keep his commandments."

> Psalm 78: 4-7 "We will not hide them from our children, shewing to the generation to come the praises of the Lord, and his strength, and his wonderful works that he hath done. For he established a testimony in Jacob, and appointed a law in Israel, which he commanded our fathers, that they should make them known to their children: That the generation to come might know them, even the children which should be born; who should arise and declare them to their children: That they might set their hope in God, and not forget the works of God and keep his commandments."

Obviously, God cares about His reputation!

Not only does God care about His reputation, He guards it carefully. There are many incidents recorded in the Bible where God takes a particular action or refrains from action "for His name sake." In fact, several times while the children of Israel were in the wilderness, they turned away from God's directions to them in ways that legally could have resulted in their immediate demise! The records of these events can be found in Exodus, Psalms and Ezekiel.

One example of these occurred when Moses was on Mount Sinai receiving the Ten Commandments and the directions for building the tabernacle. Because he was gone so long, the Israelites became very nervous. In their fear and stress, they reverted to what they had seen in Egypt and built a golden calf to worship, hoping that this new "god" would help them. God was furious with them, and basically told Moses He was ready to wipe out the rebellious lot and start over with Moses. Exodus 32:10 tells us how close the Israelites were to destruction, "Let me alone...that I may consume them: and I will make of thee a great nation."

Moses' response to God has been the subject of much query and discussion: Who was Moses to contradict God? In my view, Moses exhibited the same confidence in God that we saw earlier in our other heroes when he reminded God of how that course of action would look to the Egyptians and also reminded Him of His promise to Abraham, Isaac, and Jacob. Exodus 32:12, 13 tells us that Moses "besought the Lord his God and said, Wherefore should the Egyptians speak and say, For mischief did he bring them out, to slay them in the mountains, and to consume them from the face of the earth? ... Remember Abraham, Isaac, and Israel, thy servants, to whom thou swearest by thine own self and saidst to them, I will multiply your seed as the stars of heaven, and all this land that I have spoken of will I give unto your seed and they shall inherit it forever."

In Ezekiel we get an even clearer picture of why God didn't give the rebellious house of Israel what their actions called for:

Ezekiel 20:13-14, "But the house of Israel rebelled against me in the wilderness: they walked not in my statutes, and they despised my judgments, which if a man do he shall even live in them; and my Sabbaths they greatly polluted: then I said, I would pour out my fury upon them in the wilderness, to consume them, But I wrought (acted) for my name sake, that It (my name) should not be polluted before the heathen, in whose sight I brought them out." For His name sake, He preserved their lives.

Think about that for a minute. It isn't surprising, is it, that God doesn't want His name polluted before the heathens? Even today.

Psalm 106: 7, 8 confirms God's desire to preserve his reputation. "Our fathers understood not thy wonders in Egypt; they remembered not the multitude of thy mercies; but provoked him at the Red Sea. Nevertheless, he saved them for his name sake, that he might make his mighty power known."

Psalm 78:7, quoted earlier, gave us insight into why God was so concerned that His reputation should remain intact: it was so His people would set their hope in Him. I'm confident that He is still concerned with His reputation today, and for the same reason. He still wants us to have hope.

AUTHORITY
"STOP, IN THE NAME OF THE LAW!"

If you recognize that command, you were probably raised, as was I, in the days of cheesy Saturday morning westerns. The familiar scene on the black and white television would usually involve a runaway bad guy, dressed in black and pursued by a sheriff—the latter wearing a white hat and wielding a Colt six-shooter. The small badge on the sheriff's vest was all that indicated he wasn't acting on his own authority, so he shouted his command, "…in the name of the law!" Somehow, the words didn't sound quite so corny back when John Wayne ruled the West.

Of course, John Wayne, as sheriff, wasn't operating in his own authority, but, actually, every name carries a degree of authority with it. This aspect of our name is one which we pretty much take for granted. In fact, we might not even think of it this way, but every time we sign our name on a document we are using or expressing our authority.

There are many reasons, or bases, for our authority. One obvious one is that we have authority over that which we own. For instance, we recognize that we can make decisions about our homes that someone else cannot make. Our name on a title deed is recognized as giving us authority over property that we own. Our name on a bank account says that we are the only one who can legally access the funds that belong to us.

We also recognize that we have authority over those things or people within the realm of our responsibility. For example, as parents, our authority over our children is related to our responsibility for their welfare. Once, when Gillian was about five or six, she and her little friend, whom I'll call Amy in order to protect the guilty, were playing in our backyard. The lawn was covered with playhouse paraphernalia, including Gillian's baby bathtub. Hearing the girls' giggles, I recognized something in their tone that told me, "Check this out!" I looked down on them from my upstairs bedroom window, and, horrified, saw what they were gleefully piling into that bathtub. Gillian and Amy were in the adjacent yard stripping my neighbors' pride and joy, their gorgeous rhododendron bush, of every last blossom it owned! I screamed and ran downstairs and outside to rescue whatever was left on that shrub from the hands of my own little pride and joy. I sent Amy home and Gillian to her room to meditate on the gravity of her transgression.

Later, Amy's mother called to say, "You aren't going to tell your neighbor who did this, are you?" I assured her I would leave Amy's name out of it, but told her that when our neighbors returned from work Gillian would be going next door to admit what she had done and to ask for forgiveness.

Even though I thought Amy should share Gillian's consequence, I had no authority to ensure she did. I wasn't responsible for Amy; her mother was. I was responsible for Gillian, and I knew my authority over her couldn't be separated from my responsibility for her training. I knew this was an incident that required that I use my authority over her to teach her how to accept the consequences of her actions.

I doubt there's a parent reading this who has not, at some time, told one of his or her kids, "It doesn't matter what your friend's parents allow her to do. They're not responsible for you, so they don't get to make decisions that affect you." It's a popular and very appropriate speech!

All authority, whatever its reason or origin, can be transferred or delegated. For example, as parents, we routinely give teachers and babysitters a limited measure of authority over our children. We recognize that someone else can access the money in our bank account if given our power of attorney—delegated authority. And we all know that, when we vote, we delegate authority and, with it, the power and responsibility to exercise that authority.

THE NAME ABOVE ALL NAMES

I think one of the most touching photographs of the late United States' president, President John F. Kennedy, is one in which he is looking thoughtfully out of the window of the oval office during the Cuban missile crisis; it always underscores in my mind the awe-inspiring connection between authority—even delegated authority—and the responsibility for its correct use.

If the name of a man on this earth can hold such great authority as does a leader of a nation, and his signature affect action that can shape the world, we can only barely imagine how much authority is in the name of I AM, the Almighty God!

Psalm 24:1 tells us, "The earth is the Lord's, and the fullness thereof; the world and they that dwell therein." Why does He own the earth? Verse 2 tells us why, "For he hath founded it...and established it." We know ownership gives authority. God owns what He's created, He has authority over that which He owns, and He has the right to delegate that authority where He wishes. In the New Testament we see an example of His delegation of that authority. It is found in the name above all names.

The name of Jesus is "the name above all names". The phrase often refers to His authority, the origin of which is indicated in these verses:

> Philippians 2:9-11 (referring to Jesus) "Wherefore, God has highly exalted him, and given him a name which is above every name: that at the name of Jesus every knee should bow, of things in heaven, and things in earth, and things under the earth; And that every tongue should confess that Jesus Christ is Lord, to the glory of God the Father."

> Ephesians 1:15-22 "Wherefore I also, after I heard of your faith in the Lord Jesus Christ, and love to all

the saints cease not to make mention of you in my prayers; that the God of our Lord Jesus Christ, the Father of glory, may give unto you the spirit of wisdom and revelation in the knowledge of him: the eyes of your understanding being enlightened; that ye may know what is the hope of his calling, and what the riches of the glory of his inheritance in the saints, and what is the exceeding greatness of his power to us-ward who believe, according to the working of his mighty power, which he wrought in Christ when he raised him from the dead, and set him at his own right hand in the heavenly places, far above all principality and power, and might, and dominion, and every name that is named, not only in this world but in the world to come: and put all things under his feet, and gave him to be the head over all things to the church."

It's clear in these verses that "the name" refers to the authority given to Jesus by His Father. Jesus had taken upon Himself the form and position of a man to die in man's place, and now, because of His obedience unto the death of the cross, He was exalted in authority and power by God the Father.

According to Philippians 2:9-11, Jesus' name has more authority and power associated with it than any other name that is named, in Heaven, on earth, and under the earth. Not only does He have the authority or the right to rule, He also has the power, or the ability to rule; His Father has placed Him above all other "power and might."

In Mark 16:17, we see Jesus commissioning His disciples and giving them the authority to use His name: "In my name shall they cast out devils." We recognize that He was telling His disciples to go, not in their own right or power to rule in the situations they encountered, but in His right and power to rule. He was delegating authority.

In Acts 3, we see Peter acting on Jesus' word. He said to the lame man at the gate of the temple, "What I have I give thee: In the name of Jesus Christ of Nazareth, rise up and walk."

Notice that Peter refers to something that he, himself, has! He said, "What I have, I give thee." Peter recognized and used the authority and power he had been given in Jesus name. Later he says, "His name, through faith in His name, hath made this man strong."

KNOWING THE NAME

Having successfully completed the first stretch of the journey, we're well on our way. We're getting closer, now, to the first part of our goal—being among those who know God's name—because the more we know of the meaning of the words used to communicate with us, the greater our understanding of what is being communicated!

So how far have we come on this road? We have seen that one's name refers to identification, reputation (which includes knowledge of character, acts, and abilities), and authority. Someone's name automatically carries with it all of the above—everything he has said, done, or failed to do; his power or impotence, and even the perception of what is in his heart and at his core. These are absolutely connected and won't be perceived separately, even though in common usage the word "name" can refer to each aspect separately, as we are about to see.

So now then, equipped with the knowledge of all that is in a name, when we read these following verses about God, we may read them like this:

> Psalm 9:10, "They that know thy name (authority, almighty power, and righteous character), will put their trust in thee."

Psalm 76:1, "In Judah God is known: his name (reputation) is Great in Israel."

1 Samuel 17:45, "I come to you in the name (authority and power) of the Lord of Hosts, the God of the armies of Israel, whom thou hast defied."

John 17:6, "I have manifested (made to be seen) thy name (character, authority, and power) unto the men which thou gavest me out of the world."

Mark 16:17, "In my name (authority and power) they shall cast out devils."

In many other Bible verses that refer to the name of the Lord, we could insert the words character, reputation (which would include knowledge of His power and assets) or authority and not destroy the meaning intended even though there may be more intended than just these.

For example, God's character and reputation are indeed excellent, exalted, enduring, and worthy, and His authority exalted and enduring forever, as seen in these verses:

- Psalm 8:1 Excellent is thy name in all the earth.

- Psalm 148:13 His name alone is excellent.

- Isaiah 12:4 His name is exalted.

- Psalm 72:17 His name shall endure forever.

- James 2:7 His name is worthy.

In these following verses, which describe our proper response to His name, we could replace the word "name" with "character and reputation" and not destroy the understanding or change the meaning of the verses. In some of the verses we could replace "name" with "authority" and it still would be true. For example, we should trust His character; believe in His reputation, and fear, or reverence, His authority.

We are told to:

- Know His name. Psalm 9:10
- Fear His name. Psalm 86:11
- Believe in His name. John 1:17
- Trust in His name. Psalm 33:21
- Praise His name. Psalm 113.1
- Remember His name. Psalm 20:7
- Call upon His name. Psalm 116:13
- Hold fast His name. Revelation 2:13
- Publish His name. Deuteronomy 32:3
- Declare His name. Psalm 22:22
- Make His name to be remembered. Psalm 45:17

So then, when we publish, remember, call upon, or believe in the name of the Lord, we're making known, remembering, calling upon, and believing in His position, His authority, His power, and all of His reputation as known by His mighty acts. We're declaring, remembering, and trusting in His goodness and loving kindness, His holiness and justice, His wisdom and strength, and all of the other wonderful attributes of His character.

I should note here that in proclaiming the name of the Lord, we are proclaiming, as well, His revelatory names which we mentioned in Trail One. We should know, trust, publish, believe, and hold fast to the names by which He has revealed His covenant relationship with us.

I've always thought of words as being "fat" or "lean" depending on the depth of understanding we have of their meaning. Now that the "name of the Lord" is fatter, or, if you prefer, richer in meaning for us, it will be easier for us to see which aspect of the name is being used in Psalm 138:2. We have a nicely paved road ahead of us. The chase continues!

Thinking About Chapter Three

SELF DISCOVERY QUESTIONS:

1. Do you know someone whose reputation is without flaw? What does this tell you of his/her character?

2. Have you ever made a decision specifically in order to preserve your reputation? Why did you do that?

3. What are the areas in which you have authority? Where does that authority come from?

4. Who has authority over you? Why is that authority there?

TRUTH CHASER'S PRAYER:

Dear God,

You are my very own Father, and I'm getting to know how wonderful You are. I'm so thankful to be Your very own child! Please help me make right choices so that my reputation will never bring shame to You. May my life bring glory to Your great name.

CHAPTER FOUR

ABOVE ALL THY NAME

"Suit the action to the word;
the word to the action."

WILLIAM SHAKESPEARE
Hamlet

4.

"...for thou hast magnified thy word above all thy name." ~Psalm 138:2

As a teacher of English grammar, my days were all about how we use words to communicate. Although in my lesson plans sentence construction always took precedence over philosophy, I tried to establish in my students a respect for words and their importance to the human experience as carriers of knowledge and understanding. As we continue our search, let's remember it is God who has given us this ability to formulate, speak, and understand words. On our chase, we would be wise to take with us a great respect for His gift, and use it with honor.

Now that we have several different ways of looking at the word "name" in context, we can have another look at Psalm 138:2, this time with a clearer concept of what it may be telling us.

"I will worship toward thy holy temple, and praise thy name for thy loving kindness and thy truth: for thou hast magnified thy word above all thy name."

In this verse, the second "for" indicates that the psalmist is praising God because of something He has done. The passage is quite explicit about the fact that the writer is praising God because of His treatment of His word: He has magnified His word above all His name. It would appear that this magnification of His word above His name has shown the psalmist something of God's character that is praiseworthy; it shows him God's loving-kindness and truth. For that reason, whatever conclusion we come to about the meaning of "the magnified word," it must somehow show us these attributes of God's character.

If we don't understand—as the psalmist obviously did—what this magnification of the word means, then it's possible that the part of God's character that it reveals may remain unknown to us. If we haven't clearly seen this part of our Father's heart, then maybe we won't trust Him as we should.

Well then, let's examine it. How can God magnify His word above all His name? We have seen that a name not only identifies one person as distinct from others, it also carries with it the knowledge of one's reputation and therefore the perception of one's character. It refers, as well, to the authority and power of the person who carries that name. It's also evident that in different contexts the word "name" can refer to any one or all of these different aspects of one's name. Now our challenge is to recognize which aspect is used in the context of Psalm 138:2.

Let's look at the passage in this way:

"Thou hast magnified (lifted up, exalted) your word above all your identity."

"Thou hast magnified (lifted up, exalted) your word above all your character."

"Thou hast magnified (lifted up, exalted) your word above all your reputation."

Is it making sense yet? I'm sure it isn't. In this context, it's difficult to understand how God could magnify His word above His identity, His character, or His reputation. If He could, what would be its significance? How would it reveal His truth and loving kindness?

In this instance, could the correct use of the name refer to God's authority? Let's see how this application of the word "name" would sound in this sentence:

"Thou hast magnified (lifted up, exalted) your word above all your authority, your right and power to rule."

Could God possibly magnify, lift up, exalt, or elevate His word above His very right to rule? If so, would this mean that when God has given His word, He won't allow His right to rule to ever overturn His word?

A better question might be: Would a God of loving-kindness and truth do anything *but* elevate His word above His right to rule, or His right to do as He wishes?

Think about it! Shouldn't we all magnify our word above our right to do as we wish? Don't all people of integrity do that? The quote at the beginning of this chapter is taken from a scene in Shakespeare's *Hamlet* where Hamlet is giving instructions to actors about how to act, but, really, shouldn't we all suit our actions to our words?

But fairly often, we don't. I am reminded of a time some years back when, as thanks in response to a favor, some friends invited my husband and me to lunch at one of the finer restaurants in town. Naturally, we accepted the gracious invitation, and a date was set. On the day of our lunch date we received a call saying that they would have to postpone. Something had come up; could we rebook? We did, of course, understanding the demanding nature of the man's profession. It wasn't a problem. However, it happened again several times! By then, we were feeling very uncomfortable about going out with them at all and, sad to say, were making a mental note to avoid doing anything else for them that would obligate them to thank us with an invitation to lunch! We did finally "do lunch" and had a nice time together; however, even though the episode involved something as inconsequential as lunch, and even though it was no doubt an isolated incident and in no way indicative of normal behavior for these two, for a while —and I'm not proud of this—it made a difference in how we viewed them.

It's epidemic in our society: we don't take our words seriously. Our actions show that we are only halfheartedly committed to our words when we speak them. We write our word in a contract and sign our name under it, symbolically upholding our word with our authority; then we look for loopholes in contracts we have signed. Many lawyers are proud of their ability to get clients out of a contract, and no doubt become quite wealthy because of the marketability of such a skill. In fact, probably most of us will admit that we sometimes think of backing out of a commitment or a promise as being within our rights and not indicating any weakness of character; it just indicates that we have changed our mind.

In case you've been thinking unkindly of the friends I mentioned previously, I must remind you that we all live in a world where, sometimes, it is impossible to keep our word because of our inability to control all circumstances. At times, circumstances beyond our control make it impossible for us to fulfill our verbal commitments or our contracts. In some cases, we may have spoken the words in haste, not realizing that we couldn't fulfill them, and in others—yes, every now and then—something more important comes up. For all these reasons and more, we accept the premise that we have the right to change our minds, and indeed, sometimes must do so.

But, unfortunately, here's the problem, and here's the reason I brought my sad little lunch story up to begin with: We tend to think God does the same thing!

We think a God who sees all and knows everything can surely know if, or when, it's best not to fulfill something He has said! We presume that this lack of action on His part would be for our good because we know He loves us. We say, "After all, God is sovereign," and we expect that His sovereignty is working for our good, even if it appears His promises were not fulfilled.

God's sovereignty is, most certainly, good news to Earth dwellers, but what exactly do we mean when we say God is sovereign? Again, an examination of the word itself, separate from religious connotation, might be helpful. Webster's New Dictionary says it is an adjective, meaning "supreme, possessing absolute authority within a given sphere." When used as a noun, it refers to the person who possesses that authority.

When we refer to a country as a sovereign state, we're saying that the people and government of that country have the exclusive right to rule in that country. A king is called the sovereign because he has acquired, by some means, the right to rule in a specific geographical area or over a specific people group. Sovereignty, then, is absolute authority or the right to rule.

If Psalm 138:2 is saying that God elevates His word over His authority or right to rule, is it possible, therefore, that it is actually saying that God's very sovereignty upholds His word and will never overrule His word?

Let's think about that for a minute.

There is a verse in the New Testament that lets us know how God wants us to treat our words. It may give us a clue about what kind of value He puts on words. James 5:12 tells us to let our "yes" mean "yes" and our "no" mean "no." He wants us to mean (hold fast to) what we say and say what we mean (what we intend to hold fast to).

If we exalted our word above our right to rule our own lives, then maybe James' directive would be fulfilled. Maybe then we would "swear to our own hurt and change not," as we're directed in Psalm 15:4. Certainly, we would at least be very careful what we allowed to come out of our mouths!

Think about this: If God instructs us to have that regard for our words, can He then have less regard for, or commitment to, His word? Numbers 23:19 tells us that God is not a man that He should lie. This means that, unlike us, God can be and is committed, firmly and irrevocably, to His word. That's why the Psalms declare that God's word is forever settled in heaven. His word is not temporarily settled, merely until He has a better idea or until He gets more information or changes His mind on a whim. The psalmist says in Psalm 119:152, "Concerning thy testimonies, I have known of old that thou hast founded them forever."

Could God possibly have known when He spoke His promises that He would always, forever, be willing and able to fulfill them?

I'm pretty sure Jesus thought so.

In His famous pre-homegoing prayer for us, his disciples, Jesus refers several times to God's words. In John 17:8 He says, "For I have given them the words which Thou gavest me," and again in verse 14, "I have given them Thy word." Jesus had given His disciples lots of words—words about His purpose, about who He is and why He came, about their calling and how they were to live, and about so much more. All of these words, according to Jesus, were what He heard His father saying. In the gospel of John, chapter 8, verse 28, Jesus says, "When ye have lifted up the Son of man, then shall ye know that I am He and that I do nothing of myself; but as my Father hath taught me, I speak these things." Jesus obviously felt God's words would bear passing on to us and would stand throughout all time!

Think of it: Would God, who is all knowing, all powerful, and all wise, and who knows the end from the beginning, speak any words without absolute knowledge of their worth and of His willingness and ability to establish them all? Of course not!

Unlike us, He is not handicapped with ignorance, incompetence, or selfishness. When God spoke, He did so knowing His words were wise, good, fitting, and true for any generation to whom He sent them, and any ears for which they were intended, even yours and mine.

Let's look at our verse again.

> Psalm 138:2 "I will worship toward thy holy temple, and praise thy name for thy loving kindness and for thy truth: for thou hast magnified thy word above all thy name."

It is easy to see why the knowledge that God upholds His word by His very authority and power would cause the psalmist to praise His name for His loving kindness and truth. The psalmist is saying, "I praise Your great name, God, because You will not say one thing and do another. Your great integrity shows me You are full of truth. You will not allow Your right to rule to overrule Your word; this shows Your loving kindness to Your people." He is saying that God's integrity is the reason He will never allow His authority and power to override His word. Because of His integrity, His sovereignty will always uphold His word!

Is it difficult to get your mind around the thought that God's sovereignty will always uphold His word? If so, please don't dismiss the thought yet.

First of all, think of the implications! How would it change our lives if we expected that God's sovereignty was upholding His word? Would that knowledge be at all important in our relationship with God as we walk this earth? Might it even affect the choices we make and the things we attempt to accomplish?

Just think for a moment about God's actions "for His name sake." God was careful that His actions toward the children of Israel be in line with words He had spoken, His promise to Abraham, Isaac, and Jacob that their children would be blessed. Also, since He had sent Moses to deliver His people from the bondage of Egypt and expressed His intent before the heathen, He would not go back on His words and have His reputation, His name, polluted before them by destroying this stiff necked and disobedient bunch!

Why do you suppose that was? We know God can do whatever He wants; the earth and everything in it belongs to Him and is, therefore, ultimately under His authority, so why would He make decisions and act "for His name sake"?

Perhaps it was for our sake.

Maybe it was because He wanted to ensure that whenever He spoke, He would be believed. He wanted to make known, not only His power—he could bring the children of Israel out of bondage and into their promised land—but also His integrity—he would not abort the mission.

God had great plans for His children but He knew that if His children didn't know His integrity, they would not believe Him, and if they didn't believe Him, they wouldn't obey Him. If they didn't obey Him, they could never be or do all that He wanted them to become and accomplish.

I learned that fact of human nature when I was teaching ten-year-olds. I found out very early on in my teaching career that I had better be very careful what I said. I learned I should never say anything to these youngsters that I couldn't make good on, and if I wasn't absolutely sure that I could carry out a particular promise, then I had better establish that fact up front. Whenever these kids felt I couldn't be counted on, their frustration caused them to become discouraged and distrustful, and as a result, class control and a positive learning environment were affected adversely—actually they were "out the door." If I ever lost my students' trust, I had to work very hard to win it back.

If it was important that my students know my integrity, then surely, it's important that we, God's children, know His integrity. God doesn't expect us to trust Him without knowledge of His integrity—His faithfulness to uphold and fulfill His words. It's clear that, in the verse from Daniel 11:32, "They that know their God shall be strong and do exploits," the "knowing of God" must include the intimate, experiential knowledge of God's integrity. Again, in the words from Psalm 9:10, "They that know thy name will put their trust in thee," included in the knowledge of God's name is the knowledge of His integrity, the knowledge that He has, indeed, exalted His word above His name.

Think again about Abraham, David and the three Hebrew children. Is it possible that their knowledge of God's integrity could be the source of the confidence of our heroes of faith?

If Abraham knew God's integrity, that might explain why he expected Isaac to return down that mountain with him. He would have reasoned that since God had said that Abraham's progeny would spring from Isaac, and Isaac was not yet a father, then Isaac would have to continue to live, in order to fulfill the word God had spoken. Abraham knew that God's authority and power would uphold His word, and, because of that, he believed Isaac would live even if he offered him as a sacrifice. He knew God's right to rule would not overrule His spoken word; He had exalted His word to that extent. He is a God of integrity; therefore, His right to rule would uphold His word!

If David knew this about God, then perhaps it was the source of his confidence to stand before Goliath without a cringe. Maybe he was not merely presuming success based on his previous history. After all, history doesn't always repeat itself and this might be one time it didn't! No, it's clear that David carried more than presumption, five stones, and a sling into that battle. David carried a confidence in God that told him his enemy would flee because that is what God had said would happen. He expected smitten enemies and that's what he got! He expected God's power and authority, His right and ability to rule, to uphold His promise that He would "cause thine enemies that rise up against thee to be smitten before thy face...and flee before thee seven ways."

If Shadrach, Meshach, and Abednego knew the integrity of God, maybe that is why they could say that God can and God will deliver. Their reverential fear of God was obvious in their refusal to eat the king's meat and in their refusal to bow down to the gods of that land. They knew that God's covenant with them said that if they feared Him, angels would stand guard round about them to deliver them. They expected God to uphold His word! They knew that God's right and power to rule would ensure their deliverance. God's name was greater than Nebuchadnezzar's name. God's word was backed up by more power and higher authority than was Nebuchadnezzar's word. Nebuchadnezzar was no match for their God! God could and would fulfill the covenant. He had the authority and power to uphold His word, and His integrity would guarantee that His power and authority would always uphold His word.

All of these great exploit-doers knew that God had exalted His word above all His name. That is, they knew God's integrity and because of it they had a simple trust in God and great faith in His words.

But how might the stories have gone if they hadn't known?

What might have happened if Abraham, instead of saying, "We will return," said, "I will return," because he thought God had changed His mind about Isaac being the one from whom the promise of nations would spring?

What might have happened if David had thought he might be going to Goliath in his own name, his own authority and power? What if he hadn't expected to be backed up by his covenant God that day on that field? Would he have gone at all?

What might have happened if the three Hebrew children really *had* said, "God may not deliver, because you just never know what God will do"?

Conversely, what might happen if we really believed that God would always back up His word? What if we all expected God to do what He said? What if we expected that the very sovereignty of God would be the upholder of His word and the guarantee of its fulfillment? Would we be more willing to act on the mustard seed faith that is in us now and see it grow?

AS GOOD AS HIS WORD

Don't we all love someone who is as good as his word? There's such comfort in knowing such a one; even more in having a friend who is like that. It is an especially great blessing to be married to someone like that, as am I!

If knowledge of someone's—indeed, anyone's— commitment to his word is comforting, then knowing that the God who created this universe is committed to His word should be very comforting, indeed!

However, it also presents serious questions about events that happen in this life.

I know many of you are asking right now what has gone wrong when it's obvious that what God has promised or what He has expressed as being His will doesn't come to pass. Every day and everywhere we see things that are opposite to what God calls good. All we have to do is watch the news or even look around us. We probably don't even have to look far from home! I'm sure almost every person reading this has some painful memories of circumstances or events that fit that description—the opposite of good.

I've been there and I'm convinced that God doesn't consider our questions to be evidence of lack of faith. He doesn't get angry with us or offended. If he did, he would surely have given up on me long ago! Some of my prayers have been prayed when I was frustrated, angry, and downright fed up. I'm not going to tell you about those right now; I just will say from experience that God's word and God's integrity can stand up to scrutiny, and God doesn't want us ignorant but responds with kindness and mercy to every seeking heart. Even the hurting ones.

Like Job. I've learned a lot from reading Job's story, although I must confess he really used to get on my nerves. I think it was because when I was a child the only sermon I heard from the book of Job was based on the verse where he says, "Though God slay me, yet will I trust him."

As a child, I was uneasy when I heard it. As a teenager, I thought, "Really, Job, could you possibly have made it any more difficult for the rest of us?"

It was tough enough growing up the fourth girl in my family without having to live up to Job. I thought my three older sisters were spectacular. I often wished I were more like them: Sylvia, the beautiful perfectionist; Emmie, the gregarious intellectual; Marilyn, the free-spirited adventurer. The sisters definitely were hard acts to follow, but Job was worse. My sisters at least had the decency to have a few endearing flaws. But not so Job. I really didn't like Job. I thought he was altogether too perfect!

That is, until I finally read the book for myself. When I did, I found out that even Job prayed a few frustrated prayers—like the ones in Chapter 10: "Shew me wherefore thou contendest with me." What do you have against me, God? And, "Wherefore hast thou brought me out of the womb?" Why was I ever born?

Sounds to me as if Job was a bit of a truth chaser himself, albeit a bit of a whiner who lived so circumspectly he thought he was pretty near perfect. In fact, throughout much of his book we hear Job telling his friends that he doesn't know why God has done these terrible things to him, since he's always lived such a good life. Shades of "I don't cuss and I don't chew"?

Job's three best friends, his so-called comforters, try to help him by suggesting that Job must have done evil, or these things wouldn't have happened. Job doesn't buy it and not too patiently tells them they're wrong—that God obviously treats the righteous and unrighteous alike, since he, himself, is righteous and he appears to have ended up with the same result the wicked get! (Remember, in Malachi God says He doesn't appreciate this kind of talk; it's called "stout against God." In Chapter 3, verses 13 and 14 say, "Your words have been stout against me, saith the Lord. Yet ye say, What have we spoken so much against thee? Ye have said, It is vain to serve God: and what profit is it that we have kept his ordinance and walked mournfully before the Lord of hosts? And now we call the proud happy; yea, they that work iniquity are set up; yea, they that tempt God are even delivered." So, obviously, God couldn't have been thrilled with this part of Job's speech.)

On and on, the debate and the misery continues until even Job's wife—maybe tired of the whining, or perhaps just wanting to get rid of "the boys"—tells him to go ahead and curse God and let God kill him because of it. Maybe she, too, thinks he has earned this mess!

The only person who consistently makes good sense in the book, and the only one that doesn't get a rebuke from God for speaking "words without knowledge," is young Elihu, who waits until all his elders have finished speaking and then basically says, "Job, get your eyes off yourself. Get them on God. See who He is." Then he goes on to give a wonderful description of God in Chapters 33 to 37.

You know the story. God finally speaks for himself. The end result is that Job turns to God, sees Him as his redeemer and his help, and says, "I have heard of Thee with the hearing of the ear (perhaps implying misinformation), but now mine eye (accurate knowledge, at last!) seeth Thee." Even though Job spent most of the book justifying himself instead of God, I believe God met him right where he was because God knows that honest seekers of truth are, in fact, seeking Him. And Job was an honest seeker.

To seekers, I would give one caution in the words of a very wise pastor. Pastor Bill Johnson from Redding, California, said he refuses to let what he doesn't know interfere with what he does know.

For example, we may never know why specific tragedies happen. The reasons or, more accurately, causes may be as varied as the events themselves. In fact, we shouldn't even try to judge why tragedies, troubles or failures happen to other people. It's not really any of our business; the issues of their lives are between them and God.

Trying to understand the life issues of others may simply result in our judging people based on scriptures that were "meant for us to live by ourselves, and were never meant for us to judge others by," as my wise daughter informed me one day when I was ranting about a fellow Christian who had let me down. Even worse, trying to understand someone else's circumstances may result in our deciding that perhaps sickness, abuse, tragedy, and loss were part of God's good and loving plan for that person. Both of these may bring us to the wrong conclusions and damage us and others around us.

The truth is we don't and can't know someone else's walk with God. That's why we are told to work out our own salvation, not someone else's, with fear and trembling.

So, what are we to question? Where are we to search for answers? We all instinctively know there must be answers, even if we think we'll get them only when we get to Heaven.

Certainly, if we are to have answers here on this earth, we must go to the only truth that is absolute and unchanging. That truth is found in the scriptures that have to do with what God has said about Himself, about His plan and purposes, and about us. Our beliefs have to be formed by these, and not by any personal conclusions we come to—outside of God's truth—about the things we see happening around us or even to us. When we're surrounded by mountains and giants, we would be wise to think on the good things we know, the things that God has already called truth.

Sound familiar?

Philippians 4:8 says, "Whatsoever things are true, honest, just, pure, lovely, and of good report; think on these things." One of these good things that we should think on is the truth about the magnified word that we have just now discovered, that God has magnified His word above His name.

Thinking About Chapter Four

SELF DISCOVERY QUESTIONS:

1. Have you ever known someone you couldn't trust? Why couldn't you trust him/her?

2. Have you ever felt that God's sovereignty meant that He may not do what He says?

3. What circumstances or experiences have made you think this?

4. Are you willing to examine something you have always believed to be true, and see if it stands up to scrutiny?

TRUTH CHASER'S PRAYER:

My Father,

I confess that I have a lot of questions. This journey is not as easy as I thought it might be. Thank You that You are holding my hand and will not let me lose my way, as long as I stay close to You and listen to the voice of Your word. I do trust You, dear Father, because I know Your heart and I'm beginning to know Your ways.

CHAPTER FIVE

GOD'S GOOD NAME:
The Foundation for Trust and Faith

"Good name in man and woman, dear my lord,
Is the immediate jewel of their souls:
Who steals my purse steals trash;
'tis something, nothing;
'Twas mine, 'tis his,
and has been slave to thousands;
But he that filches from me my good name
Robs me of that which not enriches him
And makes me poor indeed."

WILLIAM SHAKESPEARE
Othello

5.

"A good name is rather to be chosen than great riches, and loving favor than silver and gold."
~*Proverbs 22:1*

A good name is the only foundation for trust. We started out looking at our ancient heroes of the faith because their lives showed evidence of a trust in God that indicated they knew His name. Apparently, their knowledge of God's good name and all that it entails instilled in them such confidence in God that it resulted in their seemingly steely resolve to obey His commandments, even to putting their very lives and all they loved on the line in the face of apparently ridiculous odds.

One reason we have had trouble relating personally to that kind of extreme trust—beside the fact that we haven't thought on His name very much!—is that we commonly use the words trust and faith as if they mean the same thing. We often use them interchangeably in our conversation. However, if we're going to walk confidently with God, we need to understand how the words "trust" and "faith" are used in Biblical context. In that context, although they are connected, they are not the same.

Consider these differences.

TRUST

Just think about your physical eyes again. Imagine walking blindfolded. How confident is your walk when you don't know where you're going? Not very, you say? Why not? It's very simple. Confidence, or trust, is based on knowledge. The Bible says so! We saw it earlier:

> Psalm 9:10 "They that know thy name will put their trust in thee."

Psalm 9:10 confirms the fact that our ability to trust someone is directly related to what we know of that one's character. Sometimes we're asked to trust someone whose actions don't portray trustworthiness. For any of a number of reasons, we may feel obligated to trust in these cases, and so we decide to do so. Actually, our will is always involved in trusting as it is in everything else we do, but deciding to trust where there is no basis for trust—little or no evidence of good character—is effectively gambling.

Sometimes, because of circumstantial necessity or because we love someone, we decide to gamble on him or her, and we call it trust. However, real trust is based on knowledge.

Well, then, what do we know of God that should make us trust Him? We have learned a lot about God's character: God is good and merciful; God is faithful and kind; God is loving and gracious. All of these lead us to trust Him.

We also know that God is sovereign. That is, He has the right to rule all His creation. We saw earlier that Psalm 24: says, "The earth is the Lord's and the fullness thereof; the world and they that dwell therein," and He, therefore, has authority over what is His.

Ah, there's the rub!

Tradition has told us that because God is sovereign, all that happens in this world has received His approval. If actions create reputation, and they do, then someone responsible for—or even approving of—everything that happens on this earth will develop quite a reputation! If we believe that all we see happening around us has passed through God's administrative desk, then His reputation will be affected adversely by it all.

Many of us, confused by the discrepancy between what we see around us and what we read in the Bible, get some degree of comfort from the thought, "God is in control." Because we know God is good, we assume that the tragic things that occur do so for a good reason. We suppose that the sickness, poverty, abuse, and death must have some measure of good if God allowed it, because we trust that God will do right.

Still needing comfort and assurance that all is well, we read books that are intended to help us be at peace with a God who doesn't seem to do what His own word would lead us to expect Him to do. These well-intentioned authors basically tell us to trust God's love and His wisdom; that is, to trust in the character of God, accept whatever happens as being His will for us, and learn to embrace the adventure. And so, because we know in our hearts that we should be able to trust God, and because we desperately want to overcome—even if just emotionally—the troubles that dog us, we try to trust.

We try, but soon we find we have difficulty putting shoes on that kind of trust. How do we walk it out? What, specifically, does that trust give us to walk toward?

Perhaps more importantly, what does it cause us to do with what God said in His word, even if we do manage to attain a measure of peace with the God the authors describe?

We must never disregard His word.

Even though trust in the character of God is right and good and wonderful because He is trustworthy, we can't please God if that attempt to trust causes us to let go of even one word He has spoken, because, according

to Him—or at least according to the Apostle Paul—the
words God has spoken are the source of our faith.

FAITH

Where do we get faith?
Romans 10:17 says "faith cometh by hearing, and
hearing by the word of God."

Why is it important?
Hebrews 11:6 tells us "Without faith, it is impossible to
please God."

What is its purpose?
Hebrews 10:38 makes it clear that "the just shall live by
faith."

Isn't it interesting that the Bible does not say that the
just shall live by trust? It says the just shall live by faith.
Trust is a foundation for faith; there will be no faith
without trust, but trust alone is not complete without
faith. Remember, trust is based on what we know of
character. Faith, on the other hand, according to Romans
10:17, is based on words. If we think about our own
relationships we will see how true that is.

I know a few good men and women. They are
people of good character and I trust them without
reservation. They're not only good people; they also
love me, and I am confident that they will never
intentionally do anything to harm me. I trust, also, that
they would only ever have good plans for me. However,
even though some of them have the means, or the
power, to pay off any debts I might have, I can have no
faith that they will do that. I know their goodness,
integrity, love, and power; and, yes, I trust them; but I
don't have faith that they will pay my debts. Why not?
Because they have never said they would. However, if
they *said* that they would, I could and would have faith

that they would do it, because I know their integrity and can trust them because of it. Faith would come by knowledge of their words, as trust came by knowledge of their character.

In the same way, we may know that God is good, loving, and kind, and that God is sovereign—that He has all the authority and power to rule—but we can have no real expectation of any specific action on our behalf unless he has said something to that effect.

For example, we may be aware of God's love and mercy, but we still could never have faith for the new birth if He hadn't said that it was available to all who would believe. Neither could we have faith for that salvation if we didn't *know* what He said about it. We easily recognize that fact as the reason for the Great Commission: Go ye into all the world and preach the gospel. Apparently, an individual's knowledge of the promise of salvation is crucial to its fulfillment in his or her life.

In much the same way, knowledge of the other promises of God is crucial to their fulfillment in our lives. For example, when we know that God is good, we'll trust in His goodness; if, however, we are also convinced of His integrity and have His word that He is our healer, and that "by the stripes of Jesus" we were healed, then we can have faith in that word and hope for it to be fulfilled. Similarly, if we who are experiencing lack know that God says He'll be our provider and meet our needs, then we can have faith in that word and, because of it, hope for the future. Likewise, if we feel lost in life and yet know that God says He will give wisdom to those who ask unwaveringly, we can take courage and expect that God will direct our paths. We can then have hope that we will eventually know the next step to take.

Real trust will always give birth to the kind of faith that holds fast to the words of the one trusted.

Real faith holds fast. It has to. For some reason, it seems, in the justice system of the universe, faith must be tested. Therefore, like the heroes of the faith we looked at earlier, we often have to hold fast to those words in the face of some very contrary circumstances!

In our examples of Abraham, David, and the three Hebrews, we see they all held fast to God's words in severely trying times. Not one of them thought Him unpredictable! They apparently considered Him to be absolutely trustworthy and His word a secure, unmovable foundation for their faith. They didn't in any way express, "God I trust You; therefore, I won't expect You to keep Your word in this instance." No, their knowledge of God's character enabled them to believe His word and act on His word, and that word was established, not only for them, but also for many others around them.

Does that kind of faith seem unattainable? Unrealistic? Unreasonable?

Don't misunderstand me. I'm not suggesting for a moment that these guys didn't ever waver or lose courage. They probably did. Even though the Bible doesn't tell us this happened, I can imagine Abraham walking up that mountain fighting thoughts of taking his son and running. But Abraham knew God, and even though there may have been horrible pictures in his mind of what was ahead, he must have been too convinced of God's faithfulness to His word to run away from His command. He probably didn't know exactly what God was up to, or why this command was given, but he had already walked with God for many years, and he knew God kept His word. That's what he was counting on as he climbed his mountain.

Maybe, when they smelled the smoke from the furnace, the three young Hebrew men had to encourage each other in the promises that were the basis of the hope expressed in "our God can and will...." As they felt the heat of the flames, they may have struggled to hold on to the confidence in God that would strengthen their resolve not to bow to a false god. We aren't told they did, but it's possible.

Then there's David. Actually, we really don't get any sense of David wavering in front of Goliath. To be honest, I'm pretty sure it didn't occur to him to hide behind a bush that day and whimper, "Oh dear God, what have I done?" Although we might be tempted to put that down—as his elder brother probably did—to the arrogance of youth, we have to remember that, even though a young boy, David had already seen God keep His promise to deliver him from his enemies. He had already seen the lion and the bear bite the dust, so he knew God was faithful. His confidence wasn't presumptive. History shows it wasn't misplaced.

Still, we shouldn't presume any of their actions were easy; as we have noted before, they were all human, just like us. Unmistakably human. In fact, Abraham and David, whose lives we follow longer than the three Hebrews, often are found to be struggling in their faith and going back to God with questions and, often, repentance. We often see them, just like us, having to be picked up and helped out of the messes they made. Their humanity, like ours, is always painfully obvious.

In the end, however, all of them, to a man, spoke and acted in ways that show us they firmly put their faith in God's promises, and trusted and obeyed His directions. This, even though at times their threatening circumstances made their faith look unreasonable and foolish and maybe even a little too blind.

However, real faith is never blind; real faith sees. Faith sees the faithfulness of the One who spoke the words from which faith came! Faith sees what was promised and experiences real peace and joy about it before it is seen by natural eyes.

Faith often may feel blind because of all the things we can't see and don't know. Here's an illustration of that. The school where I taught in Texas had a beautiful new campus just outside of town. Because there were no street lights, it was very dark out there at night. The grounds just behind the playground were very rough and uneven, and there were felled trees, small creeks, and other dangers to one who might be walking in the dark of night without a light. If, however, while trying to make my way through that dark place, I had someone who could see the way and could tell me where to go, I could walk safely in the dark by faith in the words of that person.

Jesus said His sheep hear His voice, and they won't follow the voice of a stranger, but I've learned we need to cultivate our listening skills. Most of the time, the words we listen to will be those passed down to us in the Bible. In fact, reading His written word with a heart to obey is what sharpens our listening skills. His voice then becomes more recognizable when we hear it as the still small voice of the Spirit we hear in our heart—the unbidden thought that we know didn't come from our own intellect and that is always in agreement with the principles laid down in His written word.

This little story illustrates what I'm trying to say. When our family moved to Texas, part of our funding was a forgivable loan from the university where my husband had been teaching. We were told we would have to pay taxes on the full amount of the loan when it was forgiven. While we were still in Texas, I started praying about the money we were going to need to do that when we returned home. We surely didn't have it right then and I knew we wouldn't have time to save that amount before it became due! One day as I was praying, I heard that little voice say, "That's taken care of. You won't have to pay those taxes." Later, I told my husband, "I don't think we're going to have to pay taxes on that income," and told him why.

Being the ever-practical business professor, he gently reminded me of a fact of Canadian life: If you receive income, you pay taxes—unless, of course, you have enough money to find some "shelter" somewhere. We didn't.

He did agree that we could trust God to meet our need and, somehow, provide the money when we needed it. That was good enough for me, so I left it alone and didn't revisit the possibility that we wouldn't have to pay taxes.

When we came back to Canada and received that gigantic tax bill, I went to praying! As I had learned to do by now, I reminded God of what He had said in His word about meeting our needs, thanked Him for His willingness to do that, and I let Him know I was holding fast to that word. I was shocked when I heard that voice again: "I told you that was taken care of. You won't have to pay those taxes. Be thankful for that." Not those words exactly, but the clear impression of that fact.

Of course, I told my husband. A wise and, therefore, cautious man, he decided his next step would be to go to Revenue Canada to see what method of payment they might suggest, since at this point—no matter what I had heard—we still owed them money, and had none, just having finished an expensive doctoral program!

Revenue Canada, predictably, didn't care that we had no money, and suggested a bank loan. Discouraged, Glenn went back to his office where he found this note on his desk: "Glenn, I overheard you talking about your tax bill and I thought you might be interested in this."

Attached to this note from a fellow professor—a tax lawyer—Glenn found a release from The Canadian Taxpayer regarding the non-taxability of monies given to employees for the purpose of higher education. The reform it described was in response to a court case involving an employer who felt his employee shouldn't have to pay the tax on such a monetary benefit. Interestingly, the court case was undertaken in the same year that I first heard that small voice in Texas. That note and its happy attachment made a believer out of my husband. I think he decided I wasn't crazy after all.

There's a lot more to this story; however, I will just tell you that although we both had to hold on to that word from God for two more years, and even though for all that time no one but us agreed with what God said, in the end we were able to do a "happy dance" in our kitchen when we finally held in our hands the tax bill with a lovely zero on the bottom line. We didn't have to pay the tax!

God has ways that we know nothing about. He just says, "Believe what I say, and act accordingly."

Faith, then, is believing and acting on the words of someone whose integrity we know and whose character is worthy of trust, even when we can't see one step ahead of us. Didn't Jesus say "Blessed are those who have not seen and yet believe"?

Abraham didn't yet see Isaac raised up, but believed and climbed a mountain to sacrifice his only son.

David didn't yet see Goliath smitten, but believed and ran to a giant with stones in a sling.

The three Hebrew children didn't yet see their delivering angel, but believed, refused to bow, and walked into the flames.

And out of the abundance of God's word in their hearts, their mouths spoke:

"The lad and I will return."

"This day I will smite thee!"

"Our God can and will deliver us from your hand, O King!"

INTEGRITY

Integrity is the element of one's character that provides the surest foundation for trust and faith. In someone who has integrity there is wholeness: That person's thoughts, words, and actions will be of the same "stuff." From what we have seen of our Bible heroes we can tell that they all must have been assured of God's integrity—that His thoughts, words, and actions would all look the same. We need to be assured of it too. Why? Because it is an absolute fact that we will never have faith in, or hold fast to, the words of someone whose character we perceive to be flawed, no matter how much we try. Even if that perception is incorrect or subconscious, it will cripple our trust and weaken our faith.

We all, perhaps, can think of someone, maybe even one whom we love dearly, whose word doesn't seem to be his bond. It may be a father who says yes to a request just to get some peace and quiet from persistent nagging, but without any intent to follow through. It may be a teacher who promised some special favor but backed out when it became too difficult to do, or a husband or wife who doesn't fulfill a promise because, after all, it couldn't be helped.

We do try to understand, and most of us are very forgiving, especially to those whom we love. But after a while—if it happens too often, and in spite of the love we have for those who don't keep their word—we really don't have a lot of faith in what they say.

In spite of the love we have for God, if we really don't think His word is His bond we won't rely too heavily on what He says. And, sadly, because we attribute to Him the responsibility for all the terrible situations that we see around us, and because those situations are not what His word describes as His will for us, we are often unsure of His faithfulness to fulfill His words, even though we believe Him to be loving and wise. Because we have held the erroneous belief that God's sovereignty may overrule His word, our confidence in the integrity of our Father has been crushed. Then, tragically, even though we have an unshakeable belief in our salvation and a firm expectation of eternal life in Heaven, our reality is that we sometimes live our lives on earth as though God has spoken nothing more than His promise of eternal life through faith in Jesus. The reason for this is as simple as it is clear: We won't hold fast to any of His words that we aren't sure He holds fast to as well. We may think we should and we may try to, but we won't.

I wonder if that's why we sometimes don't seem to find the time to read the Bible, or, when we do, it's merely so we can feel good that we have checked off a duty and have hopefully pleased God by doing so. Perhaps it's because we don't really think the Bible is relevant to our everyday lives since we think we can't count on it. As a result, we go on living wordlessly.

But, surely, we can know God upholds His word! We know that when God says something to humankind, He has the power and authority to bring it about. Because His word is exalted above His name, above His very sovereignty, we know He will not change His mind. His word has become law to Him as well as to us. That's probably why He calls His word, "Forever established!"

What a comfort to know someone keeps his own rules! In *The Voyage of the Dawn Treader,* the fifth book in C.S. Lewis' *Chronicles of Narnia,* Aslan the Lion—who many literary critics suggest represents Jesus—delivers a great line to Lucy when he appears to her in response to her use of the Magician's book. When Aslan tells her he came because of what she did, she's disbelieving because she thinks her actions can't possibly affect a response from the great Aslan. She says, "As if anything I could do would make you visible!" Aslan replies, "It did. Do you think I wouldn't obey my own rules?" (159)

What a picture of God's integrity!

God holds fast to His own words; that's integrity! We hold fast to His words; that's faith! His sovereignty, His right and power to rule, assures us that God is able. His word and His integrity assure us God is willing.

Daniel 11:32 says, "The people that do know their God will be strong and do exploits." I'm convinced people who do not know God's integrity will be, at best, weak and do little. Why? Because if they don't know His integrity, they can't be fully convinced that God will stand by His word, and they will do only what they know they can accomplish on their own, without the power of God to back them.

THE CURRENCY OF THE KINGDOM

My father, an avid reader and lover of the Bible, once told me, "I'm starting to believe that faith is the currency of the kingdom." I think he may have been right.

Somehow, in the legal system of Heaven and this universe, belief is a necessity, not only belief in God's existence, but belief in His words. In Isaiah 7:9, the prophet Isaiah had been sent with a message from God to Ahaz. It was good news; his enemies' plans would not come to pass. But God also told Ahaz, "If ye will not believe, surely you will not be established."

Believe what?

Believe the message Isaiah had brought!

It is amazing that, even though God had spoken what was to be, He required Ahaz to believe it in order for it to be established! God, who had all the authority and all the power needed to manifest His promise, was saying, "Ahaz, if you don't accept My words, it will be to you as if I didn't say them."

I know it seems incredible that such a thing could be. We are, after all, talking about one who is truly sovereign. Surely, you may say, God's words don't need man's acceptance in order for them to come to pass! I'm inclined to agree. But they do when He says they do! And often He says they do.

We see the truth of that repeated too often when people reject the gospel. God has sent His word in John 3:16. He tells us right there, in black and white, that He loved us so much He sent His son, Jesus, to carry the sins of the whole world and pay the death penalty required. The Bible doesn't say He *will* put our sins on Jesus. It says He has already done so. Yet, if people don't accept God's words, it is *to them* as if He said nothing.

A savior has provided salvation for every man and woman born on this earth, and yet, if they don't believe, it will be *to them* as if nothing has been done. The life-giver came, but if He's rejected, death prevails. Light came, but if that light is rejected, darkness prevails.

It remains, for some, as if Jesus did nothing.

In the same way, if we, as Christians, let go of or fail to hold fast to any promise that God has made, it will be *to us* as if He had not given it. It will be *to us* as if the words had never been spoken.

Ephesians 2:12 speaks to this issue: "At that time ye were without Christ, being aliens from the commonwealth of Israel, and strangers from the covenants of promise, having no hope and without God in this world." When Ephesians refers to being strangers from the covenants of promise as being "without hope and without God," it is saying that in living without the promises we are living "practically godless" lives!

This truth is tragic: If we believe that God's sovereignty may overrule His word and, therefore, subconsciously think we can't trust God's integrity, then we certainly will live life in much the same way as strangers from the covenants of promise, even though we are blood-bought, church-going, Bible-reading children of God. We will, then, certainly think that the faith of the Bible heroes is unattainable, and maybe even rather ridiculous.

Throughout the Bible, we see our dear Father trying to get across to us the necessity of believing His words, even when that belief looks unreasonable. I say "looks unreasonable" because it's never unreasonable to have faith in God. It's unreasonable not to.

Just as the Bible tells us the just shall live by faith, it also tells us that it's by faith and patience that we receive the great and precious promises we have been given. If these two statements are true, then we can see why an understanding of Psalm 138:2 would be so important to us. It lets us fix our hearts on a fixed word.

THE LIGHT IN A DARK PLACE

We live in a dark place, as dark as that school yard in Texas. Psalm 23 tells us that though we walk through the "valley of the shadow of death" we need fear no evil. That valley is life on this earth. From the time we enter this earth as tiny vulnerable babies until the time we leave, we're shadowed by the dark presence of death.

That presence has been here almost since the beginning. In this bright and beautiful home that God created for His family, where Adam walked clothed in glory, there was a tragic day when the light went out. We have all heard about it. On that horrible day, when Adam chose to act on the words of the rebellious angel, Lucifer, he effectively became his servant and put God's enemy in charge on this earth, and the sovereign God—because He is righteous—had to honor his action. The glory left, and Adam, horrified, realized that he was naked and vulnerable.

We can't quite imagine what it was like for Adam and Eve to live in glory, but we do know that on the day the glory left, death began its reign of terror, and we all know how it feels to live in its shadow. We have lived with it ever since, and I dare say that every fear we have can be traced back to our fear of death.

Why does Psalm 23 tell us that, even on this earth where death and darkness must be allowed to remain for a time, we need not fear? It's because "Thou art with me." Adam's sovereign and righteous God had provided a remedy: the light, Himself, is with us.

There are actually two representations of light found in the Bible. The first is Jesus. Isaiah, prophesying about the birth of Jesus, said in Isaiah 9:2, "The people that walked in darkness have seen a great light: they that dwell in the land of the shadow of death, upon them hath the light shined." Jesus, himself, said in John 8:12, "I am the light of the world; he that follows me will not walk in darkness." Zacharias, John the Baptist's father, speaking of Jesus coming, said, as recorded in the book of Luke, "The dayspring from on high hath visited us, to give light to them that sit in darkness and in the shadow of death, to guide our feet into the way of peace."

The second representation of light is God's word. In Psalm 119:105, the psalmist says, "Thy word is a lamp unto my feet and a light unto my path." Later in the same psalm he says, "the entrance of thy words gives light; it gives understanding unto the simple."

How else do we follow Jesus, the light, if it is not by receiving, believing, and walking by faith in His words? If we don't, or if we can't because we don't know God's integrity, we still walk in some measure of darkness. Certainly, God's word can be a lamp and a light only when we believe it; it will benefit us only when we act on it.

Interestingly, the scriptures also tell us that we *live* by two things: God's word and faith. Jesus said that man shall not live by bread alone but by every word that proceeds from the mouth of God. We saw in Hebrews that the just shall live by faith. As they say in Texas, these two, faith and the word, are tied together with a very short rope!

We read earlier that without faith it is impossible to please God. Have you ever wondered why that is?

There may be many reasons for it, but one seems obvious. If it is, indeed, by faith—and patience, don't forget; there's the holding fast again—that we receive His promises fulfilled, then we can see why it's impossible that He be pleased with less than that! That's one reason it is so important that we understand the integrity of our God, who exalts His word above His authority and upholds His word with all that His name represents: It will strengthen our trust in His character and our faith in His words.

At about six in the afternoon on September 11, 2001, after a day filled with tragedy and uncertainty, a worried Karen Hughes, counselor to President George W. Bush, finally was allowed to return to her White House office where she found an e-mail from the pastor of the church she had attended back in Austin, Texas.

Pastor Doug Fletcher assured her of his love and prayers and those of her fellow congregants at Westlake Hills Presbyterian. He included notes from the meditation on Psalm 23 that he had given in services that dark day.

Pastor Fletcher wrote: "Christian faith doesn't suggest that life is easy …The empty cross, a symbol of victory, is also a reminder of evil and violence. There are valleys, some of them dramatic and some of them less so. We do need a shepherd in these valleys. And we are not simply promised a safe journey. We are promised a banquet. It is one thing to live bravely underestimating the danger. It is another to understand the dangers and live with the confidence of faith in the promises of Him who promised never to leave us or forsake us." (243, 244)

Surely, just as any father would be, He is pleased and honored when we believe what He has promised.

Thinking About Chapter Five

SELF DISCOVERY QUESTIONS:

1. Do you think God has a good reputation? Why? Why not?

2. Can you trust Him? Why? Why not?

3. Can you have faith in what He says? Why? Why not?

4. If the answers to the above were negative, are you willing to change your opinion?

TRUTH CHASER'S PRAYER:

Dear Father,

I am willing to see my own heart. I am willing to change in any way that pleases You. Open the eyes of my understanding so I will know if I have not believed something You have told me.

PART TWO:

Our Response

CHAPTER SIX

LESSONS FROM
SUNDAY SCHOOL
AND TURTLES

"The light of the body is the eye:
therefore when thy eye is single,
thy whole body also is full of light."

JESUS
Luke 11:34

6.

THE PARABLE OF THE OKLAHOMA TURTLE

Actually, this isn't really a parable. It's a true story, but, like a parable, this story has in it a lesson to be learned. A few years ago, early on a quiet spring morning, I was driving home from Tulsa, Oklahoma, with my daughter who had just graduated from university. We were the only car on a long stretch of highway. Gillian was sleeping and I was enjoying the beautiful Oklahoma countryside when I saw what looked like a rock in the middle of the road. I kept my eyes on it, wondering what it was, and as I got closer I saw it was a turtle making its way across the highway. Just as I was thinking, "Oh, how cute! It's a...," I felt a horrible bump. You know it! Tragically for that little guy, I went right where my eyes were looking.

I think of that little turtle whenever I find myself focusing on places I really don't want to go.

It reminds me of a chorus we sang in the little country Sunday school I attended as a child. It went like this:

Oh, be careful little eyes what you see
Oh, be careful little eyes what you see.
For the father up above is looking down in love,
Oh, be careful little eyes what you see.

At the time, in Sunday school, I thought the song was about not displeasing God with what I looked at. However, after my Oklahoma turtle encounter, I believe the reason for its message is this: We really do tend to go where our eyes are looking!

Of course, I'm not the first to have noticed that. My friend, Judy, recently told me about vacationing with her family at a dude ranch in Arkansas where she, along with her husband and two children, took horse riding lessons. One of their instructor's favorite directives was "Don't look down! Look where you want the horse to go! You go where you look." Arkansas turtles are safe with that instructor.

Consider this: Every day we naturally look straight ahead when we walk. It's easy for us to recognize the difficulty and danger of walking when we can't see where we are going. Our physical eyes are so enormously important that the very idea of living without them is horrifying to us.

As well as our physical eyes, we also have a "mind's eye." The Bible calls it "the eyes of our heart." As we are meditating, or thinking, we are actually mentally seeing something. Just as physically we can, and do, purposely look toward the place we want to go, so we can, and must, deliberately place our mind's eye on where we know God has provided for us to go. How? By meditating, or "thinking on" those good things mentioned in Philippians 4:8.

Meditation on God's love, God's word, and God's right and power and faithfulness to perform His word, will bring a resurgence of hope for the "goodness of God to be seen in the land of the living." On the other hand, meditation on the Goliaths of life and the reasons for our own weakness or inadequacies, will deplete our expectation of God's involvement in our battles, and possibly annihilate our courage to fight.

Remember our story about Abraham? He didn't spend his time wondering why God had asked him to sacrifice Isaac or worrying about his own inadequacy to produce another son. Even though he must have had the same emotions any father would have at such a request,

Abraham kept his inner eyes on "in Isaac shall thy seed be called." We don't hear David talking about Goliath's size or complaining about the apparent cowardice of the rest of the people of covenant. He kept seeing "The Lord shall cause thine enemies to be smitten before thy face." There's no record of Shadrach saying to Meshach and Abednego, "What went wrong? Why are we heading to certain destruction? Does God want to deliver us from slavery this way, by this terrible death?" No, I believe they kept seeing the words written over one hundred years before, "Thou shalt not be burned." From the record we are given, we can see that they all kept their focus on the covenant word of their God, and His faithfulness to establish that word. They kept their eyes on God.

We really do go where we're looking. There's evidence of that everywhere. Our family has traveled and lived in several different cities because of my husband's career. This lifestyle brought with it the opportunity to see up close many local church bodies. It's always easy to see the beauty of Jesus in every one of these churches; it's sometimes just as easy to see how we lose our way.

At one time we attended a church where the statement of faith would include divine healing, the indwelling of the Holy Spirit, and God's provision for His people. However, the pastor, with the best of intentions, I'm sure, spent much time preaching about why much of the church is sick, powerless and poor. It wasn't surprising that there was a pervasive atmosphere of sadness in the church. They looked too long on failure! We need to be realistic and accurate in our assessment of any situation we're in, but our focus must remain on God, not on ourselves or people around us.

An observation of another church gives us an example of the danger of looking too much at our own efforts. I noticed that, at times, when it seemed—to me, at least—that the people were most unified in expression of praise and worship, the leader would exhort the congregation, reminding them that there were higher heights to be attained in worship. This exhortation always resulted in a stronger vocalizing of praise which would last for just a minute or two. Then, almost as if tired by the exercise, everyone would shut down, and the spirit of worship that had earlier pervaded the atmosphere simply disappeared!

When I noticed that this scenario repeated itself often, I began to watch for it. Sure enough, it happened every time: praise, interruption and shutdown! For a while, I puzzled over why this would be. I knew these people. They weren't a rebellious group, so why wouldn't they follow through on the leader's instructions? I finally concluded, rightly or wrongly, that the reason for this phenomenon was their change of focus. Perhaps before the exhortation the "eyes"—or thoughts—of the congregation were on God. Maybe afterward they focused instead on their performance in worship. There will be no argument that true worship can only flow from one whose eyes are on our wonderful Father.

I tell you those stories just to say this: In the same way, true faith can only be released when our eyes are on God and His strength and faithfulness. Faith will be impeded when we look too much at ourselves, or our circumstances. It is interesting that, in the story of Job, it was after Elihu's admonition that Job should get his eyes off himself and onto God that God shows up and turns Job's captivity. In the previous examples of Abraham, David, and the three Hebrew children, we saw that no matter what was going on around them they kept their eyes on God's promise and His right, ability and willingness to perform what He had said.

When we were in Texas, while my husband was a doctoral student and making very little money, I was teaching in a private Christian school. It was a great blessing since it provided not only funds desperately needed to keep body and soul together, but it also provided meaningful work and beautiful friends.

Unfortunately, it didn't provide pay during the summer months when school was out, and because I was an alien in that country, I couldn't just go get a job anywhere. In accordance with immigration rules, my work had to be in my profession and my would-be employer would have to go through months of paperwork and red tape to get me approved. For someone to do that for a few months was unreasonable, even if I had been allowed to work at something outside my field for a couple of months. The result of all this was that, for the summer months, my budget was short about $800.00 each month. Not a lot of money, except when you don't have it! For the first time in my life, it looked as if I would have to choose between eating and paying the rent. No matter how I looked at it, I couldn't figure out how to come up with the cash, short of begging, that is. I had never done that before; it seemed downright unbecoming to a Christian. And, besides, who knew if it would work?

In all my meditating on my predicament, my only hope came from the Bible, specifically the book of Philippians. Philippians 4:6,7 says, " Be careful (full of care, my paraphrase) for nothing; but in everything by prayer and supplications, with thanksgiving, let your requests be made known to God, and the peace of God, which passeth all understanding (which is not based on what you can see and know, my paraphrase) shall keep your hearts and minds through Jesus Christ." And Verse19 was a life-line: "My God shall supply all your need according to his riches in glory by Christ Jesus."

In order to maintain my sanity, I continually kept that word before my eyes! I would like to say I didn't give another thought to my husband's and my inability to provide for our family, but it wouldn't be true. I thought about it all too often because I'm a bean counter at heart and love to manipulate numbers, but my numbers just would not be manipulated with any happy result! Thankfully, every time I went down that road and came to the same dead end I would remember what God had said. I knew that had to be my bottom line. I had already learned, long ago, that He would back up what He said, so I would just remind myself, over and over if I had to, that I could believe Him, even though, right at that moment, I couldn't see where on earth the money would come from—so He was on His own with no help from me!

And provide He did. Eight hundred extra dollars each month.

The first month's extra funds came as a result of a car accident I had been involved in just a few weeks earlier, when someone on the parking lot of the university backed out of his spot and into the side of our car as I was driving by. When the other driver's insurance company interviewed me, I told them I was physically unharmed by the accident and that I had received an estimate of $400 for cost of repairs to my car, which, of course, I had. The interviewer asked, "So then, will $1100 be enough?" Thinking that American insurance companies were considerably more generous than their Canadian counterparts, I agreed that the amount would cover things nicely, and a few days later I had their check!

When we told a friend at church about our good fortune, not only was he surprised at what the insurance company had allowed us, he also said, "It shouldn't cost $400 to fix your car. I'll take you to my guy. He'll take care of you for much less than that." True to his word, he did, and his friend did "take care of us" for much less. We came away from the whole transaction with— you guessed it—an extra $800, just what we needed for the first month of summer vacation.

I won't bog you down with the details of the following two months because there are a lot of details, including overbooked hotels that paid for accommodations elsewhere, universities that gave overly generous honorariums, and three days' work turning into a few hours' effort! It's enough to say God has his ways! He kept his word in ways that I couldn't have imagined! And because of His grace and goodness, we had $800 over and above our regular income each month of the summer and on into the first month I was back at school.

Would that have happened if we hadn't kept our eyes on what God said about being our provider? We'll probably never know. I know one thing for sure: I would have had no peace at all. There's more about that in the next chapter, but why should we even care to find out what would happen if we left God out of life's equation? Isn't it better just to do what He said and let Him keep our hearts and minds in peace? Better just to believe Him and keep Him before our eyes?

In the book of Hebrews, chapter 12, the apostle Paul writes to some people who appear to be having a crisis of faith. He chastens them a little because, he says, they should have been teachers by now, but he has to teach them again about who Jesus is and what He did for them. At the end of the book he gives them some advice about how to keep the faith and run their race with patience: Look unto Jesus, the author and finisher of our faith.

When I was a teenager in church we sang a chorus that went like this:

Turn your eyes upon Jesus.
Look full in his wonderful face.
And the things of earth will grow strangely dim
in the light of his glory and grace.

When I sang that song back then, I thought it meant that things of earth weren't important to God, and, therefore, shouldn't be to me either. I don't think that way now. Now I realize that many things of earth are very important to God, especially those things that are part of our fulfilling our destiny.

What this wonderful song says to me now is that when we keep our inner eyes on Jesus, when we see His goodness, wisdom, and power, and when we know His favor and eagerness to show Himself strong on our behalf, then the things of earth, such as the giants and the mountains—and the lack of $800 a month—will be put in proper perspective. We'll see them as small in the light of His glory.

Ah, His glory! His love and mercy, goodness and grace, integrity and faithfulness, justice and power!

Oh be careful, little eyes, what you see!

Thinking About Chapter Six

SELF DISCOVERY QUESTIONS:

1. Is there something you are looking at right now that you don't want to move toward?

2. Do you believe God wants you to go there?

3. Are there any scriptures that might lead you to a different place?

TRUTH CHASER'S PRAYER:

Dear Jesus,

You are my shepherd. Help me keep my eyes on You as I follow You. Help me to listen to the voice of Your word and to hear Your still small voice in my heart. And, Jesus, please let me know when my eyes wander.

CHAPTER SEVEN

OUT OF THE ABUNDANCE
OF YOUR HEART

"Be not deceived, God is not mocked;
for whatsoever a man soweth,
that shall he also reap"

PAUL THE APOSTLE
Galatians 6:7

7.

"In quietness and in confidence is your strength."
~*Isaiah 30:15.*

My father went to Heaven at the age of 90, early in the summer of 2003. For his home-going celebration, our family chose a bulletin with these words on the front: The Greatest Believers are the Most Patient Waiters. A successful farmer, my father knew how to sow seed, water the seed, nourish the seed, and patiently wait for the harvest he expected it to bring. He was a great believer in the power of seed.

Jesus referred to God's word as seed. As believers in God, we must know how to sow God's word in our heart, water it with praise and meditation, nourish it with obedience, and wait patiently and expectantly for its fulfillment.

As we have turned the pages of this book, you and I have been preparing our hearts to be good ground for the seed. As we have studied the name, we have come to know what our Father did when He exalted His word above His name and we can now include in our meditations this thought, "My father God holds His word in great regard. He upholds it always with His authority and power." That sweet meditation will continue to help make our hearts good soil for the seed of His word, breaking up any ground hardened by disappointment and failures, and removing stones of fear and doubt.

I'm convinced that the same thought will also help us to hold fast to the promises of God with faith and patience as did Abraham, David, and the three Hebrew children, even in the midst of contrary circumstances. Our confidence in our Father will be unshakable no matter what comes! Psalm 112:7 tells us the righteous man is not afraid of evil tidings because "his heart is fixed, trusting in God." Remember a "fixed heart" on a "fixed word"? Although God calls our belief in Him righteous, it's not the righteousness of the man but rather the integrity of the God whom the righteous man has come to know that causes the heart to be fixed.

I expect there is yet another fortuitous result of truly trusting God when we know His commitment to back up His word. It is this: The knowledge of our Father's integrity will give us the strength and courage to do His will, to go as Peter did, in His name, and make His great name known.

Remember Peter? He was the one who walked on water with Jesus simply because Jesus said, "Come." He was the one who took his eyes off Jesus, put them on the storm raging around him and began to sink! He's the one, also, who lost courage and denied Jesus on the infamous day of Jesus' trial; yet, he's the one who later said to a crippled man, "What I have I give thee. In the name of Jesus Christ of Nazareth, rise up and walk!"

Why did Peter believe he had something to give? It surely wasn't because of his stellar performance in recent days! Could it be that he finally learned to simply believe what Jesus said? He believed the words we find recorded in Matthew 16:17-18 where Jesus told His disciples what they, or "he that believeth," could do in His name. Surely, Peter must have believed that in spite of his own failures, everything Jesus' name represents would, that day, back up his words to the cripple.

Surely, you and I can believe it, too, in spite of past failures—ours and others'.

One morning, during the time I was writing this, I was spending some time praying for my family. My daughter, who was attending university in another city, had called the day before and had mentioned that her ears were blocked; she was in pain and her hearing was affected.

While I was praying, Peter came to mind. Earlier, I had been writing about Peter saying, "That name, through faith in that name, has made this man strong." Having focused for days on God's faithfulness to back up His word with His power, I now was keenly aware that just as Jesus had delegated His own authority to Peter, He had, by His own words, delegated His authority to me and I had, at that moment, the responsibility to use it! I felt sure that His power would back up my legitimate use of His name. I was convinced that the name, the character, authority, and power of Jesus would back up *my* words if, in the authority of *His* name, I would command my daughter's ears to open and the swelling to go down. So, all alone in my front room, with morning sunshine pouring through the window, I did just that!

The next day, my daughter called. I asked how her ears were feeling. She exclaimed, "It was so strange! Yesterday, at around 1:00 p.m., my ears suddenly got hot, and they began to drain! The pain is gone and I can hear fine!" I had been praying at 11:30 am, which was 1:00 p.m. in her city. That name, through faith in that name, had made her ears whole!

Has this kind of result always happened? The truth is, no, not at all.

It's also true that it happens more often when my eyes remain on God and His faithfulness to His word.

I wonder if that could be at least part of what Jesus was talking about when He said, as recorded in John15:7, "If ye abide in me and my words abide in you, ye shall ask what ye will and it shall be done unto you."

Sometimes, we have to work to regain a place where the word abides in us because, in this life, there will always be something that comes to steal the word from our hearts. For example, several years ago, when I was diagnosed with breast cancer, I realized that I had been foolishly neglectful because I had felt a thickening in my breast a year earlier, but had ignored it, convincing myself that it was my imagination! And now, when I was faced with a potentially life destroying disease, my shame over my neglect almost caused me to let go of what I knew was God's desire to be my help. My shame kept my eyes on me.

My dear friend and former pastor, Lorne Rostotski, told me, "This is threatening your life. Psalm 103:4 says that God redeems your life from destruction. Expect Him to do what He said." In other words, it's your life, not just your health, that's in jeopardy, so start looking in the right direction. Look at God's promise to deliver your life from destruction.

As I did that and, also, focused on other words that related to the circumstance I was in, the "abiding" of the word became stronger. I began to thank God for all the wonderful words He had spoken, for all the great things He had already done for me, for His often proven faithfulness, and for His loving kindness and truth. Confidence in God began to overcome shame and the fear that accompanied it, and eventually removed them altogether. I actually had the audacity, or perhaps it was just confidence in One who loved me, to ask God to redeem, or buy back, the time I had wasted. Then I thanked Him for it, before I saw it.

Shame said, "You don't deserve that," but Jesus said, "Ask what ye will."

After the surgery the oncologist told me, "You had a very well behaved tumor!" Apparently, given the size of the tumor and the history of the disease in my body, the tumor would have been expected to be much more advanced. Selah.

With a very grateful heart I thanked God; I still do today. I was very thankful for what the doctors had done, but more grateful that "the Lord taketh my part with them that help me," Psalm 118:7.

Always give credit where credit is due!

But, you may ask, how does this work? How is it possible that what we meditate on makes a difference to the outcomes in our life? We can easily understand how our thoughts can affect our choices and therefore also affect the natural results we attain in many endeavors, but how does it work when our own power is not involved? How can what we believe make a difference to our outcome when God is the only one who is able to affect the outcome—when supernatural power is necessary?

Maybe it is just as my father said; maybe faith really is the currency of the kingdom. I do know this: there are hundreds and thousands of stories of God backing up His word with His power and authority, not just in Bible times, but in our day. In all of these stories, we find some pretty ordinary people who have the faith and courage to trust and obey their great God. These stories can be ours, yours and mine, but we have to do our own trusting and obeying.

Sometimes, while we're trusting and obeying, we try to figure out how or when God will fulfill what He's promised. Big mistake. That's not our job: It's His. Ours is one we can do. Our job is to meditate on God's great name and allow ourselves to be developed in faith and courage. It may seem small, but it's powerful, and it's a vital part of our destiny.

Romans 8:29 tells us, "For whom he did foreknow, he also did predestinate to be conformed to the image of his Son, that he might be the firstborn among many brethren." Jesus walked in faith and courageous obedience, and completed what He was sent to do. We get to do the same thing. It's our privilege to do the works we were sent to do and be conformed, even in this way, to the image of Jesus.

It always surprises me when I hear people say they think their destiny is something over which they have no influence. They suppose that the plan for their lives is somehow set in stone and, good or evil, they just stumble upon it. They don't realize that even though God has a predestined plan for our salvation and has exciting works for each of us to do on this earth, we have to choose to walk out His plan.

We have been given free will, the authority to make our own choices, and we also have been given the responsibility to use that authority wisely. God doesn't set His good plan out there for us to stumble upon without volition, and neither does He spread it out for us to see as a whole and then choose or refuse. He, instead, gives us His word as a light to our path and says He'll never leave us, but will instruct us all the days of our lives.

There's a precious moment in C. S. Lewis' *The Voyage of the Dawn Treader* when Lucy pleads with Aslan, "Oh, Aslan! Will you tell us how to get into your country from our world?"

He gently replies, "I shall be telling you all the time."

All the time, day by day, God is telling us how to live in the light. We can choose, refuse, or maybe even just neglect to take him up on His offer of guidance and accept His words as truth. We choose, refuse, or neglect to walk in light. There is always a choice. We couldn't possibly have been created in the image of God but not have been given the power to choose.

The concept of choice is intrinsic in a covenant. Throughout the history of God's covenants with humans, there is evidence of Him telling us we have to choose. In the Old Testament, which is about the destructive power of sin, the people of the covenant had to choose to walk in obedience to God's laws. In Deuteronomy, when God gives the old covenant blessings and curses to His people he says, "See, I have set before thee this day life and good, and death and evil; therefore choose life." (Deuteronomy 30:15-20)

Years later, in a message to King Zedekiah—who had asked of God what he should do in the face of the besieging Chaldeans and the advancing army of King Nebuchadnezzar of Babylon—Jeremiah gives him God's reply: Their enemies will be victorious over them, but if they leave the city and fall into the hands of the Chaldeans, they will live; if they stay in the city, they will die at the hands of the Babylonians. Then he says, "Thus sayeth the Lord, Behold I set before you the way of life and the way of death." (Jeremiah 21:8). They had to choose the way they would go, and their outcome would be based on their choice.

Still today, under a new covenant, our destiny waits on our choices. The New Testament is all about the life-giving power of the grace-gift of righteousness that is received through faith in Jesus. John 1:1-5 says, "In the beginning was the Word, and the Word was with God, and the Word was God...In him was life; and the life was the light of men...and the light shines in the darkness." In this new covenant we still have to receive the gift of righteousness by our own will, and then choose to walk every day in the light that is lovingly provided.

But surely, you say, no right thinking person will deliberately choose darkness and death! You are right, of course, but some choose darkness by default. Because we still live in the dark valley of the shadow of death, we have to deliberately choose life in the same way Abraham, David, and the three Hebrew children did, by accepting God's word as light and truth and not letting it go.

It may be daunting to think our choices are so important, but, in all of this, can you see the hope you and I have? God has planned and provided for our success, not our failure! God loves us and comforts us in our failure, and picks us up when we fall, but He has planned and provided so that every one of our lives would reflect the glory of His great name. We all get to choose life!

But He won't make us do it. He won't make us trust and he won't make us believe and he won't make us obey. Obedience takes our own volition. Unfortunately, when called upon to go in Jesus' name to do His bidding, we'll go timidly, if at all, unless we're confident that we are going with the force of His sovereign right and power to rule backing up His word every time. Unless we're confident that when we take our stand on God's word His sovereign right and power to rule is upholding that very word, we will stand tentatively and not for long.

Surely, in order to be all we are called to be in this world, we need to know we aren't alone. We need to be sure that not only does God want us to trust Him, He also wants us to believe Him and to expect that He will keep His word. God knows we need that kind of confidence in Him. That's why God has let us know, through the recorded words of the psalmist, that He has exalted His word above His name: so that we will put our faith in what He has said, no matter how long ago He said it.

If what I've told you here is true, what implications does it have for your life right now? What effect will it have on your fulfilling your destiny if dealing successfully with earth's giants and mountains is part of the great and exciting works you were born to do? Can, or will, what you have read here make a difference to how you respond to the challenging giants and disheartening mountains you face?

It can, you know. As you search God's word and listen to your heart you'll find the direction you need to scale the mountain that blocks your path. Or maybe you'll cast it aside, as Jesus said in Mark 11:23, "Whosoever shall say to this mountain, Be thou removed, and be thou cast into the sea; and shall not doubt in his heart, but shall believe that those things which he saith shall come to pass; he shall have whatsoever he saith." Whichever you do, remember Jesus has already said that you have the ability to handle mountains.

The giants you face are more dangerous than the mountains. Your mountain will just sit there and, although it may keep you from moving forward or keep you from something that belongs to you, you can ignore it even while you pitch your tent in its shadow. Giants are a different matter. Just like David's Goliath, your giants are actively trying to steal, kill, and destroy. What will you do about them? How can you slay the giant that threatens your life or inheritance?

Just as David did!

The other day I watched a movie depiction of the life of David. In the scene with Goliath, they show David walking timidly toward the giant and finally stopping and staring, appearing to be somewhat mesmerized. Then, silently, he picks up a stone, puts it in his sling and lets it fly. He misses. After several tries, David, looking a little frazzled by now, manages to hit Goliath in that one vulnerable spot on his forehead.

I was disgusted! Typical of many Hollywood portrayals of Biblical events, they missed the whole point and left out the best part! Yes, David used a little stone in his sling that day, but his real strength—that the Hollywood producers didn't see or didn't bother to show us—was the confidence in God that was behind the words he boldly yelled at Goliath, "This day will the Lord deliver you into my hands!"

Isaiah 30:15, quoted under the title of this chapter, confirms that our strength is found in quietness and confidence. The confidence it refers to is our confidence in God. That confidence in God is our strength, not just to endure, but to do, to accomplish, to take care of business! So take your cue from a young shepherd. First, find out what God has already said about your giant. Then, maybe, do a little yelling of your own. As you do, you might just find at your feet some special stones designed perfectly for a giant's forehead.

I guess that's really the gospel in a nutshell: believe in your heart, confess with your mouth, and act on what you believe. Romans 10: 9, 10 told us all about it: "If thou shalt confess with thy mouth the Lord Jesus, and shalt believe in thine heart that God hath raised him from the dead, thou shalt be saved. For with the heart man believes unto righteousness and with the mouth confession is made unto salvation."

Remember that night in Ziklag, when David was "greatly distressed; for the people spoke of stoning him, because the soul of every man was grieved every man for his sons and for his daughters" and, as 1 Samuel 30:6 also tells us, he "encouraged himself in the Lord his God"? As the speaker on my tape said, the Bible account doesn't tell us how David did that. We do know he wept bitterly with the others. We know he was despairing of his life. We know, too, that he cried out to God and said, "What do I do now?"

However, I think if we look carefully we'll see he also did just what we have been talking about. I believe he readjusted his sight and put his eyes on God. Maybe he thought of the vanquished bears, lions, and giants of years gone by. Maybe he simply recalled a day, long ago, at his father's house in Bethlehem, when the prophet Samuel anointed him to be the next king. It may have been there, in remembering God's promises and His faithfulness, that David found the courage to obey the new directive God gave him and to believe the promise that accompanied it: "Go, and you will recover all."

Without doubt we know that David turned from his despair, effectively changed where his men were looking, encouraged them to pursue their enemy, and, finally, led them to victory as they reclaimed their families and goods from the Amalakites.

As you read this, you may be experiencing troubles of your own. You may be scared and even a little despairing, but, if you are, don't be too hard on yourself. After all, we just saw a man after God's own heart— killer of bears, lions, giants, and ten thousands—in trouble and scared. Just do what David did that day. Turn your eyes away from the mess around you and encourage yourself in the Lord your God.

That's what I did that cold night in February when the combination of chemotherapy drugs and antinausea drugs kept me awake yet again. One more time, I took my eyes off what I was going through, off what history said could happen, off statistics and all other distractions, and got them once more on a faithful and loving God who, as it says in Psalm 103, "redeemeth thy life from destruction." I encouraged myself in the Lord.

You can do that too. Don't even look inward to see what you may identify as "only mustard seed faith." All faith looks like mustard seed before it's planted and given time to grow and bring that mustard plant into the light of day.

No, your eyes don't belong there, looking inward; that's "all about you" again. Wrong focus! Keep your eyes on God's integrity, on the perfect love He has for you, and the word He has already given you. As you do that, your fear of giants and mountains will give way to quietness and confidence. That's where your strength lies.

How do you keep your eyes on God? My pastor has a favorite saying that makes it clear, "Read your Bible."

Good advice!

In God's word, He shows you who He is. His word also shows you who you are—who that "new creature" is that God made you to be. Without the knowledge and wisdom found there, in your Bible, you have nothing before your eyes but your giant, yourself, and whatever resources you can find around you.

But there is so much more to this world than just what you can see around you! There is faith that comes from God's word, a real force and source of power that will help you walk this valley called earth and walk it strong, with the courage to be all you were created to be.

There's an unforgettable and heartbreaking line spoken by Marlon Brando in the movie *On the Waterfront*. He says, "I coulda been a contender. I coulda been somebody." Sometimes I wonder if at least some of the tears that God will wipe away when we get to Heaven will have been there because we have finally realized, "I could have done what God wanted me to do. I could have been an overcomer. His grace was sufficient. He told me so, but I wasn't sure I could believe it."

Thinking About Chapter Seven

SELF DISCOVERY QUESTIONS:

1. Have you ever felt unworthy of God's favor?

2. Do you think it's unfair that faith might be the kingdom's currency?

3. What would be a better currency?

4. What is meant by the saying: Self-righteousness is as filthy rags?

TRUTH CHASER'S PRAYER:

Father God,
   Your ways are higher than my ways! Your way is full of grace and mercy, and Your way planned the "by grace, through faith" principle. Help me to walk in Your ways.

CHAPTER EIGHT

•————————————————————•

GUARD YOUR HEART

"The devil can cite Scripture for his purpose."

WILLIAM SHAKESPEARE
The Merchant of Venice

8.

"Keep thy heart with all diligence for out of it are the issues of life." ~Proverbs 4:23

Lenin once said, "A lie told often enough becomes truth." I'm sure he meant a lie told often enough begins to sound so familiar that we mistake it for truth, and therefore it becomes the accepted reality by which we live. In the introduction to this book, I suggested that somewhere along the way our perception of God's character has been distorted, and we haven't been aware that it has happened. It did happen, however, and it happened because we believed something that simply was not true. Unfortunately, lies don't produce life.

Where did the lies come from? Certainly, no one told them deliberately. Maybe we even thought them up ourselves; we're quite capable of doing that! We heard them, whatever their origin, and we believed them— strange ideas about God, ideas that He must be shocked at and disturbed about!

Well, okay, perhaps He's not shocked but surely He must be disturbed!

There was a funny, but still disturbing, example of one such idea in an episode of the hit sitcom *Seinfeld*. George is talking to his therapist and says something to the effect that he's afraid to be too happy because God wouldn't like that. I laughed at George, but I could understand his paranoia. I'm sure I probably thought the same thing at one time! Maybe you have, too.

I remember a saying that was common in my childhood and was often used by parents when their kids were cutting up too much: "You'll be laughing on the other side of your face before the day is out." In other words, you may be laughing now but you'll be crying soon. Perhaps that was just another version of "God doesn't like it when you're happy."

Examples of that bit of misinformation abound! The other day, after my chiropractor had adjusted my out-of-place rib, he asked how I was feeling. I answered with an enthusiastic "Great." He quipped in return, "When the good Lord sees us with a grin on our face, He wipes it off. So just say you're doing better."

There it is again!

How on earth did the good doctor and George and I believe such a thing, when God's word tells us in Proverbs 17:22, "a merry heart does good like a medicine," and Psalm 16:11, "in thy presence (God's presence) there is fullness of joy and at thy right hand pleasures forever," and much more about the subject, all of which should convince us that God, like any father, loves to see His children happy? I don't know for sure how we came to believe it, but we did, and George and I, as well as my wonderful chiropractor and probably countless others, walked for a while in a measure of darkness because of it.

There are other lies. I'll bet you can think of some you've heard and perhaps believed. Just watch a little television and you'll hear more than a few! Of course, it's just TV, just entertainment, and in many cases just a joke, but if we spend too much time away from our own reading of the Bible, the lies we hear from the media and other sources appear true.

Why does that happen? I think it may be the same reason why a field left alone, untended, will go to weed. Jesus told us His kingdom worked much like a farm. In the Bible, our hearts are often referred to as a garden, a place where God's word is sown to produce a harvest, and a place we are to guard and tend, for out of it are "the issues of life." The words we speak, and the things—good and bad—that we do, all come, the Bible tells us, from our heart.

Earlier, I mentioned the eyes of our hearts and the importance of what those eyes look at. It's in our hearts that our future is formed and that future is irreversibly connected to the picture of God that we see, or don't see, there.

The other day, a friend forwarded to me this story about a little girl in kindergarten, painstakingly drawing something. The teacher says, "Tell me about your picture." (She knows that one should never ask a kindergarten child *what* it is they've drawn; one is expected to be able to recognize what it is!)

"It's God," the little girl answers. Her teacher tells her kindly that no one knows what God looks like.

"They will in a minute," she replies.

We're so like that little girl. We sometimes draw our own picture of God, based on bits of information we have heard or based on what we have seen and experienced of the darkness of this earth and attributed to Him. Unfortunately, our picture may not look at all like God.

In the information age that we live in, knowledge abounds and is available at the click of a mouse! Misinformation also abounds and is just as available. The biggest piece of misinformation we have believed and, I'm convinced, the one that has most perverted our perception of God is one that says because God is sovereign, He reserves an "out" where His promises are concerned. We may have believed that for a myriad of reasons, but now we see that Psalm 138:2 gives clear evidence of God's integrity, that His sovereignty upholds His promises.

To clearly see God, we always have to go where He has drawn His own picture. From Genesis to Revelation, God patiently and carefully paints a picture of Himself, telling the story of His loving pursuit of His children and inviting us to know Him. Only there can we even begin to recognize who He really is. As He takes us through the scriptures from the time and place where His light and glory were bright, the Garden of Eden, through millennia of darkness where His light was small, we arrive at the turning point of time, when Jesus came and showed us the Father as He walked among us.

One day as Jesus was walking He stopped by Jacob's well in a city called Sychar, in Samaria. He struck up a conversation with a Samaritan woman and, during their chat, He tells her, "You worship you know not what…but the hour comes and now is, when true worshippers will worship the Father in spirit and in truth: for the Father seeks for such to worship him."

In other words, God wants us to worship Him with a true picture of Him in our hearts.

I'm a tad reluctant to share with you this somewhat silly account of an incident that occurred at my wedding reception many years ago, but I will, since it illustrates painfully well what I'm talking about.

A popular wedding tradition in those days was to have someone give a toast to the parents of the bride. I asked my parents' pastor to perform this duty for me, and he enthusiastically agreed. When he stood up to toast my parents, it was obvious that I had miscommunicated my request, because he began a toast to me, the bride, whom he didn't know at all!

At first I thought that all would still be well, since he was saying such lovely things; in fact, I was really quite enjoying what he had to say about me, and thought this wasn't going too badly after all, when my hopes were dashed. Here was the problem: everyone who really did know me soon thought that he was sorely deceived or hallucinating when he went on and on about what a great cook I was! I was horrified to hear not-very-well-disguised snickers from a few of my nearest and dearest friends! The loudest snicker, almost a guffaw, came from one of my bridesmaids, my former apartment mate, Gloria, who had crunched through more than one of my burnt offerings. Oh, how I hoped the pastor's praise for my culinary skills was prophetic, but time has proven that, alas, it wasn't! He just didn't know what he was talking about. It was a toast without knowledge—praise without truth.

On The Day of the Glimmer that I mentioned in Chapter One, when my heart stopped me from continuing in what I have since called fake praise, I was doing something very similar to what that dear pastor did only it was much worse. I was worshipping, or at least speaking words of worship, without understanding what I was saying. I was worshipping without truth. The words themselves were truth; they just weren't my truth. Jesus words to the woman at the well in Samaria show us that God wants our worship to spring, almost unbidden, from the truth about Him that we hold in our hearts. Only then is it true worship, the kind that one of my favorite authors, Laurie Beth Jones, has written about. She says, "Worship puts us in touch with the divine, and when we are in touch with the divine we rise to our highest and our best." (85)

Scattered throughout the Bible there are many statements of what worship does for the worshipper, and it would be a wonderful subject to study. However, not the least of these benefits is one that is obvious, and, in fact, one that Laurie Beth Jones' statement speaks to: It helps us stay focused on our Father, and helps us walk with Him. Jesus said the Father is looking for such worshippers; He wants worshipers who know Him. Let's not settle for less than what He wants.

Not settling takes diligence. Whenever I notice that strange ideas, lies about God, are beginning to filter into my thought processes, I have a check up Psalm that I go to, a sort of heart monitor. My check up is Psalm 103. It's not the only place in scripture that we clearly see God, but it is so easy to catch sight of his heart for his children there. It may be good for you to read that psalm again, just to refresh the picture your heart sees.

Not settling also takes the courageous and committed heart of a truth chaser because although truth may reach the mind by casual hearing, it doesn't settle into the heart and become functional and fruitful without personal engagement. Do you remember my first step in this process—the one Proverbs told me about? Even though we know the speaker here is a man talking to his son, we commonly accept that it is God's wisdom for us as well. He tells us, "Receive my words. Put your heart in it. Listen. Ask. Seek. Search!" Get actively involved, as you would in a search for something of great value. Search as you would for gold.

When God put Adam in the Garden of Eden, He told him there was gold there and it was good. In Proverbs, He tells us there's gold in His word and it's good. Be assured it will take effort to find it, but it's worth the effort it will take. The Holy Spirit will help us, but we must seek in order to find.

There's my pastor's advice again: Go ahead and read your own Bible. Read it carefully and prayerfully, and find its treasure. Discover its truth.

Thinking About Chapter Eight

SELF DISCOVERY QUESTIONS:

1. Have you ever been worried that God might have bad plans for you?

2. Why have you thought that?

3. Can you think of any other misinformation you have accepted about God?

4. Where did it come from and why do you think you believed it?

TRUTH CHASER'S PRAYER:

Dear Father,

Help me to recognize what is true and what is false. Please help me to find the gold. Help me to worship You in truth.

CHAPTER NINE

HOW DOES YOUR GARDEN GROW?

"Nothing will come of nothing."

WILLIAM SHAKESPEARE
King Lear

9.

"Behold a sower went forth to sow."
~*Matthew 13:3*

We crawl into bed, exhausted and sleepy. As we reach to turn out the light we see the Bible sitting reproachfully on the night table. Luckily, we know how to get rid of the guilt that just jumped into bed with us. Psalm 134 or 150—one of the short ones—will do. Or maybe even a whole chapter of Proverbs, especially if we missed yesterday's reading.

I'll bet there are more than a few of us would-be followers of Jesus who recognize that scene. There's definitely nothing wrong—in fact there's everything right—with wanting to have a daily Bible reading, but when did reading the Bible become one of our daily chores, something we have to do in order to feel as if we have accomplished all we need to do before putting head to pillow? When did it become just another demand for our time in an already crowded life? It's not supposed to be that way. You know it; I know it; all God's children know it. And God knows it! God knows we don't need another flaming hoop to jump through.

In fact, even though scenarios and feelings like those I've just described are probably too familiar to every one of us, I believe we have always known at some heart-level that the Bible was and is a gift to us—a marvelous, precious gift that is meant to benefit us. The metaphors we have been looking at that describe His word—light, gold, bread, and seed—all, and more, show us that God wants the time we spend reading His word to be more than something we do to prove our devotion to Him or to collect those infamous Brownie points. The images evoked by these words show us that His word is necessary to our very existence as Christians.

Our ability to wholeheartedly respond to God's word in the way He wants us to is what this book is all about, and as a teacher, I can't resist a review! This last chapter is a non-exhaustive look at some of the ways the very psalmists with whom we began our journey responded to God's word. Let's let them bring it all together for us—our review before the test!

Psalm 106 shows us one more time that our first response to what God says is to believe it. We read there the root cause of the set of behaviors that got the children of Israel into so much trouble in the desert was this: "they believed not his word ...and they hearkened not unto the voice of the Lord."(Psalm 106:24, 25): They didn't believe God, so they didn't do what He said.

As we read about the Israelites, it becomes clear that refusing to believe God's words will put us on a track that eventually will prove destructive. In our perfect hindsight, it's also obvious that the reverse is true. As we follow the account of the Israelite's journey through the wilderness, it's easy for us to see that believing God is the beginning of walking a right path. If you're like me, you've often wondered how the children of Israel could ever be so blind as to disbelieve; maybe it's our own blindness that keeps us from recognizing the moment *we* start walking down the same wrong road as they!

"But," I hear you saying, "I wouldn't read the Bible if I didn't believe it."

I did. I read it faithfully for years and didn't believe it.

Well, maybe I should say that I did intellectually affirm that it was true, and, certainly, I tried to live by the parts that told me things like: Don't steal; Don't lie; Don't forget the assembling together.

I definitely thought I had that first response covered. If anyone had asked, I would have said I believed, because I did affirm the veracity of the Bible. However, I only accepted and put into practice—or at least tried to—the parts that gave me something I felt I could handle on my own. Unfortunately, that list of "do's" was quite limited. The sad truth is there was a lot said in my Bible that I believed intellectually but consistently left on the night stand, on those pages between the leather covers.

But on the day I heard of my sister's heart-shattering diagnosis and prognosis, when I prayed that dangerous prayer, "I'm going to read Your word as if I've never seen it before, and I want You to speak to me through it," I found out just how much of that word I had never really believed.

I opened my Bible at the gospels and, for hours, followed Jesus on his travels. I listened to his gentle voice as He told the people, "Fear ye not, for you are of more value than many sparrows," and I knew I'd always had a difficult time accepting that.

I heard Him say, "Ask, and it shall be given you; seek and ye shall find; knock and the door shall be opened to you: For everyone that asketh receiveth; and he that seeketh findeth; and to him that knocketh it shall be opened," and I knew I had never wholeheartedly believed that, in all of my then twenty years as His disciple.

When He said to the desperate father whose young son was tormented by an evil spirit, "If thou canst believe, all things are possible to him that believeth," I had to face the fact that I had never taken those words seriously—at least, not enough to believe all things were possible to me, too, if I would believe Him.

I even thought I might have caught Him in a lie when I heard Him say, "If ye abide in me and my words abide in you, ye shall ask what ye will, and it shall be done unto you." Of course, I knew it must be true because He said it, but, somehow, it didn't seem possible to me that He actually meant it! I couldn't imagine anyone on earth having that kind of relationship with our creator.

As I sat and stared at the words on the page—"ye shall ask what ye will and it shall be done unto you"—it suddenly hit me that if there were no circumstances under which these words were true, then they were, actually, a lie! I was stunned! It slowly dawned on me that, somehow, somewhere in time, space and experience, there must be a circumstance under which these words were true! What a place that would be to spend your days! The words of the beginning phrase, "If you abide in me and my words abide in you," sent a shock through me as I realized they described that place!

At that moment, the truth chaser inside me—long buried by years of disappointment and intimidation, and long since replaced by polite apathy—was resurrected.

That occurred over twenty years ago, and since that night I've never doubted the integrity of God. I've faced giants since then and I've stared up at a few intimidating mountains. I've needed my hope renewed occasionally and my courage restored often, and there have been too many times I've failed to listen and obey, but I've never doubted that God would hold fast to His words, and I've never been sorry I prayed that prayer. The treasures it brought me have empowered my journey ever since.

You see, I found out that reading God's word is just the beginning. Even believing is just the sowing of the seed. Just like my successful farmer father, the wise sower will follow through and care for the seed until it produces its fruit.

The book of Joshua lets us know how to follow through; it shows us how to take the word with us through the day. At the beginning of the book, Joshua has been given a job to do. He's taking over the leadership role vacated by Moses, and he's getting some "how to" advice from God—how to make his way prosperous and have good success in this new endeavor. In Joshua 1:8, God says, "This book of the law shall not depart out of thy mouth; but thou shalt meditate therein day and night, that thou mayest observe to do according to all that is written therein."

In that one verse, we see three ways we are to respond to God's word after hearing and believing it. The first of these three is simple: We talk about what He said. We talk to Him. We talk to ourselves if we have to! We keep what He said in our mouth, even when it doesn't appear to be true at the moment and even when what He said we should do looks like a bad move! A key to doing this is found in Psalm 119:128, which says, "I esteem all thy precepts concerning all things to be right."

All His precepts concerning all things! That might be tough, but it's doable. It simply means we agree with God! That means when revenge looks good, we esteem forgiveness to be right. When hate feels natural, we choose to love. When we feel lonely, we esteem God to be our constant companion. When despair looks appropriate, we esteem hope to be right. When destruction looks inevitable, we esteem Him to be our deliverer from destruction. When doubt rushes in, we esteem faith to be the responsible choice. All because He said so.

Obviously, His ways are higher than our ways; His thoughts, than our thoughts! They are so much higher they may seem unnatural to us, but the next step helps with that.

The next step, according to God's advice to Joshua, is this: We mediate on what God said. The more we do so, the wiser His ways and His thoughts appear. It may sound like a practice associated with Eastern religions, but actually, if Joshua had to do it, we do too. Not to worry, though; it's easy. We meditate all day long anyway; we're experts at it. We meditate on problems at work, on challenging relationships, on health issues, on new furniture we would like to buy—on something! Meditating comes naturally. God is telling us that, in all our meditating, we must not only consider what He has said, but also make what He has said the bottom line in our mental manipulations. He definitely has said something that can relate to those problems at work, or those health issues, or difficult children. I'll wager He might even have something to say that will affect when and how we buy that furniture!

Psalm 119:24 is our next step and coincides with the third of God's instructions to Joshua. It says, "Thy testimonies also are my delight and my counselors." A counselor gives you insight and helps you initiate appropriate action, and when we esteem God's word to always be right in every situation, we are pretty close to that step where we let it be our counselor. When we hear or read the testimonies of what God has said and done in the past, those very words become prophetic of what He will do in the future. As we read His precepts and laws, they become the wisdom that directs our actions. Those testimonies, prophesies, precepts, and laws affect the choices we make in the present and, before we know it, God's word has become light to our path, and we will finally learn to "observe to do."

Psalm 119 gives us another one of the precious purposes God had in mind when He gave us His word.

In verse 52, the afflicted worshipper says, "I remembered thy judgments of old, and have comforted myself." God's word—full of stories of His just judgments, steadfast faithfulness, and promised blessing—is given to comfort us and calm us in the middle of our storms. His word can fulfill that purpose only if we read it, believe it, meditate on it, talk about it, let it counsel us, and give it time to create hope in us.

God meant for His word to be our hope builder. He meant for it to build in us an expectation of future good. In verse 49 of that same psalm, the psalmist is praying, and although it seems he's trying to convince God to help him, he actually is letting God know he's hanging on to His word for dear life, "Remember thy word unto thy servant, upon which thou hast caused me to hope; this is my comfort in my affliction: for thy word has quickened me."

God's plan is that we get hope from what He says! That's why it's so important that we know God's sovereignty upholds His word and we can, therefore, expect Him to fulfill His word; without that expectation, there can be no hope beyond ourselves. As we read God's word, believe what He said, and carry it in our heart, we'll see that, gradually, it will change not only our actions, but also our expectations. It will change what we see ahead of us; it will create a vision of what can be.

When we follow this path laid out by the psalmists, we will eventually find ourselves at a place described by verse 162 of this same Psalm, "I rejoice at thy word as one that findeth great spoil."

Great spoil! Isn't that what we've been talking about all along?

At last, we recognize the treasure!

Reading our Bible is no longer a chore; we now see God's word as the light that shows us where to walk. It becomes the necessary bread that, daily, gives us the strength to live. We begin to value its treasures as the silver and gold that bring beauty and empowerment to our walk on this earth, and we treat His word as precious because it is the God-given seed of our God-ordained future.

Can you imagine the future that will spring from that seed? Think of it: You, a successful workman that needs not to be ashamed, becoming all God created you to be, accomplishing all that He calls you to do and living the abundant life Jesus said He came to give!

Is the thought slightly disturbing?

In the book of Matthew, Chapter 5, Jesus is sitting on a hilltop, looking around at a small group of ordinary people—a couple of rough fishermen, a government worker, a couple of rowdy guys He called Sons of Thunder, and others—and beyond them, a multitude. He began to teach them some important things about light. He told them, "You are light."

They are? He can't be serious!

Yes, they are light.

Then He tells them, "Shine."

The fact that He had to tell them to shine indicates three things: shining doesn't happen automatically; they have a choice to make in regard to this light; and they could possibly choose wrongly!

Why would they make the wrong choice? Maybe they're afraid.

Our own response to Jesus' words—excitement or discomfort—may tell us whether or not we're afraid of our light.

What happens in a dark world if those who *know* the light, *have* the light, and *are* light are afraid of their light? You know the answer to that: There is nothing to dispel the darkness.

Even though most of the stories told in this book have to do with my own and my family's life, I know none of us is an island. Our lives and destinies are inextricably intertwined, and as we walk in His light we get to share that light with those who walk with us and, God willing, even those who come after. That's why we mustn't allow ourselves to be frightened by the light God gave us. We have to embrace it and share it.

But how do we get rid of the fear? And how do we shine?

We start by taking the light off the night stand. As we begin to fully respond to God's word, we fully respond to Him, and as His word becomes all He intended it to be in our lives, we'll be confident that we were designed to go higher. We will have no doubt that we were meant for more than mere survival or even for more than arriving safely in Heaven, as precious a hope as that is. We'll be convinced that even though eternal life in God's presence is our greatest goal, He has designed, purposed, and empowered us for good works and for great exploits, and for righteousness, peace, and joy on our earth-walk in His presence and in His light.

None of these things—our right standing with God, our unreasonable joy and peace in times of turmoil, nor, certainly, our good works and exploits in His name—would be possible on this dark earth were it not for the bright and beautiful truth that God has magnified His word above all His name. All of the above can come only from Him; they are all His doing. It truly is God that calls us upward.

It should be clear, but sometimes isn't, that God calls us with words. Even the impressions we receive in our heart are translated to our conscious mind as words. We're even told that we partake of God's divine nature—we experience all that He is, and receive all that

He lovingly provides—through His words. Through His precious promises.

If that is true, there's no wonder the psalmist praised God's name for His loving kindness and truth when he thought of the priceless treasure of Psalm 138:2. So do we.

On this time-encased planet, everything has a beginning. Robert Richardson, in his book *Emerson: the Mind on Fire,* says that "on a day no different than the one now breaking" (555) extraordinary things have begun. He writes about a time when the works of Shakespeare, the beauty of the Mona Lisa, and the music of Beethoven simply didn't exist. But then on some ordinary day, perhaps sunny, perhaps rainy and grey, the journeys began which led to beauty that has graced generations.

It is doubtful that those artists knew, at the outset, every line of poem or play, every stroke of brush, or every note that was yet to be. But that didn't stop them. None of the journeys were completed in a day, but aren't we glad for their beginnings?

On this very day you can begin a new extraordinary way of life, one characterized by trust in God and faith in His word. It may be a small beginning, as beginnings usually are, but from this day forward you will never be counted with those "cold and timid souls" of whom Theodore Roosevelt spoke, who know neither victory nor defeat, but rather with the valiant for the faith, who climb mountains of obedience, refuse to be cowed by fiery furnaces of persecution, and run to giants, shouting the word of their God as they go.

Go ahead; let the exploits begin.

Thinking About Chapter Nine

SELF DISCOVERY QUESTIONS:

1. Which of God's seeds are already sown in your heart?

2. What fruit do you see from those seeds?

3. Are you willing to search the scripture to find the many seeds God has provided for the good harvest that is your divinely intended future?

TRUTH CHASER'S PRAYER:

Dear Father,

How faithful and kind You are! Your presence is my joy. Your loving kindness and truth are my daily comfort. Your every word is precious in my sight. Thank You for each of them, and thank You for Jesus, the Word made flesh, who showed us Your true glory when He lived among us, and still does today. Thank You for Your Holy Spirit, my Comforter, Teacher, and Guide. With my eyes on You and my heart's ears listening intently to Your voice—and by Your grace, through faith—I'll finish, with joy, the course You've set before me.

APPENDIX ONE

When God Relents

In the story recorded in Exodus 32, where Moses
withstood God, we saw that God relented and did not do
what He said He wanted to do—that is, destroy the
Israelites and, in their stead, make of Moses a great
nation. I can imagine that some, reading this and other
stories where God changes a declared plan, might think,
"There! God doesn't always hold fast to what He says!"

In these stories, and perhaps in all stories of such
kind—for example, that of Jonah and his preaching to
the city of Nineveh—I expect we will find that God's
first declared plan of action was in accordance with His
previously established words and, therefore, a legitimate
response to the actions of the men and women involved.
His subsequent relenting was in response to the
repentance of the people or even the requests of His
servants, and, always, His new plan was in accordance
with His mercy and His well known will to restore and
do good to His people.

Another such story is that of Hezekiah, recorded in
2 Kings 20. God's prophet told the ailing Hezekiah what
the future held for him—he would succumb to his
sickness and die that very night. In this instance, as in
the others, because of God's great mercy and in
response to Hezekiah's prayer—which seems to be one
that He loves to hear: I'm hoping in Your word—God
intervened on his behalf and healed him, giving
Hezekiah fifteen more years.

So it would appear that whenever Biblical accounts
suggest God is not upholding His word, it is actually

that He is upholding His promise to forgive, to restore, and to bless when His people—even if only one in the whole bunch, as in Moses' case!—respond to Him in hope, trusting in His goodness and His faithfulness to His word.

Psalm 106 gives a clear picture of how the story goes: The children of Israel, time and time again, turned from God's wisdom, did not believe His word, complained in their tents, and did not heed the voice of the Lord. Justice required that they eat the fruit of their folly. And so they did. But time and time again, when they cried out to God, this was His response:

> Vs 44-45: "Nevertheless, He regarded their affliction when He heard their cry; And for their sake He remembered His covenant, and relented according to the multitude of His mercies." (NKJVim)

APPENDIX TWO

Different Translations of Psalm 138:2

Psalm 138:2 has been translated differently in different versions of the Bible. In some versions it appears that the translators, in their attempt to make the text more understandable to modern day readers, found it difficult to stay close to the original. While this happens rarely and is not always a problem, in some incidences where the original language doesn't easily translate into modern day usage, the paraphrase that results may be limited by the understanding of the writers/publishers or even by preconceptions based on a previously established theological bent. Therefore, I believe it would be helpful to look at the way this verse reads in several of these translations and compare each to the rendering of the text in the original language, Hebrew.

The Interlinear Hebrew-Aramaic-Old Testament; Volume III of the Interlinear Hebrew-Greek-English Bible: The literal translation of this verse: "Will I worship/ sing will I praise to you/ the gods before/ my with heart whole/ will I you thank/ your truth for, and your mercy for/ your name, give and to thanks/ your holy temple toward/ you answered me/ I call in the day/ your word/ your all above name/ have you magnified for."

The English arrangement of these words according to this same Bible: "I will thank you with my whole heart; I will sing praise to you before the gods; I will worship toward your holy temple; and give thanks to your name for your mercy and for your truth; *for you have magnified your word above all your name.*"

New American Standard: "I will give thee thanks with all my heart; I will sing praises to thee before the gods. I will bow down toward thy holy temple, and give thanks to Thy name for Thy loving kindness and Thy truth; *for Thou hast magnified thy word according to all thy name*."

New International: "I will praise you, O Lord, with all my heart; before the gods I will sing your praise. I will bow down at your holy temple and will praise your name for your love and your faithfulness, *for you have exalted above all things your name and your word*."

Amplified: "I will confess and praise you O God, with my whole heart; before the gods will I sing praises to you. I will worship toward your holy temple, and praise you for your loving kindness and for your truth and faithfulness; *for you have exalted above all else your name and your word and you have exalted your word above all your name*."

In two of these translations, the *NIV* and the *Amplified*, the phrase is rendered, *"you have exalted above all things your name and your word'"* The *Amplified* goes on to include the phrase as it appears in the closest translation to the original, *"for you have exalted your word above all your name*."

Whatever we read in the Bible must, in its essence, reveal God to us, show us what He's done, or tell us His will for man. At the very least, any words that we read, even in the Bible, must communicate something to us that is understandable and usable. Before we decide what each of these translations of our text is communicating to us, we must look at each translation of the phrase in the context of the whole thought.

The whole thought of our verse is centered on the reason for the psalmist's praise and worship. Since the psalmist is praising God for His loving kindness—also translated mercy—and truth, we know that the magnification of *"the word and the name"* or *"the word above the name"*—whichever is being communicated—showed the writer these characteristics of God.

If it is indeed *"the word and the name"* that are exalted above *"all things,"* we have to ask how the exaltation of these "above all things" showed God's mercy and truth. It may show us His power and authority, but not His mercy and truth.

The rendering in the *NAS, "for Thou hast magnified thy word according to all thy name,"* can be subjected to the same scrutiny as was the *KJV* in the text of this book by inserting the elements of a name: *"For thou hast magnified thy word according to all thy identity, character, reputation and authority."* Again, it's difficult to see what is being communicated here and what it has to do with loving kindness and truth.

Both of these fall short of communicating anything that gives us reason to praise God for His mercy and truth.

The most beautiful paraphrase of that verse that I have found and the one that is closest, I believe, to the spirit of what it is actually saying is found in *The Living Bible*. I gave a copy of that Bible to my father many years ago, and several times over the years he told me how much he enjoyed the simplicity of its message. After writing the text of this book, I was delighted to find in my father's Bible this paraphrase of Psalm 138:2.

The Living Bible: "Lord, with all my heart I thank you. I will sing your praises before the armies of angels in Heaven. I face your temple as I worship, giving thanks to you for all your loving kindness and your faithfulness, *for your promises are backed by all the honor of your name.*"

There it is: God's integrity, which is, I believe, what the text truly is all about.

References

Cahill, Thomas. *How the Irish Saved Civilization,* Doubleday, New York, 1995.

Green Jay P, Sr. (ed.) *The Interlinear Hebrew-Aramaic Old Testament,* Hendrickson Publishers, Peabody, Mass 1961

Hughes, Karen. *Ten Minutes from Normal,* Penguin Books, New York, 2005.

Jones, Laurie Beth. *The Power of Positive Prophesy,* Hyperion, New York, New York, 1999.

Lewis, C. S. *The Chronicles of Narnia; The Voyage of the Dawn Treader*, Harper Collins, New York, 1980.

Richardson, Robert. *Emerson: The Mind on Fire,* University of California Press, Berkley and Los Angeles, 1995

The Comparative Study Bible, Zondervan, Grand Rapids, Michigan, 1984.

The Living Bible, Tyndale House Publishers, Wheaton, Illinois, 1971.

The Holy Bible, New King James Version, Thomas Nelson Publishers, Nashville, 1982

About the Author

Born on the east coast of Newfoundland, Canada, Fay Rowe has also lived on the far west coast of Canada in Victoria, British Columbia, and on the not-so-far-east coast in Halifax, Nova Scotia. As well, she lived for several years in the United States while her husband attended university in College Station, Texas.

As teacher of fourth graders and junior high students, and in settings such as Sunday morning church services, Wednesday night Bible studies, seminars, and various Women's Club and conference events, Fay has shared powerful insights with people of all ages. In this, her first book, she communicates truths that have empowered a great many lives and, she is convinced, will bring those who act on them closer to fulfilling their God-given destinies.

Fay resides in London, Ontario, with her husband, Glenn, and their adopted barn cat, Casey.

●————————————————————————●

If you have enjoyed *What's In A Name: Rediscovering the Integrity of God,* look for Fay's new book, *Keepers of the Testimony,* to be released in the fall of 2007.

For more copies of this book, go to www.amazon.com, or inquire at your local bookstore.

Printed in the United States
71926LV00002B/1-84